HOME
THERAPY

HOME THERAPY

INTERIOR DESIGN FOR INCREASING
HAPPINESS, BOOSTING CONFIDENCE,
AND CREATING CALM

Anita Yokota

PRINCIPAL PHOTOGRAPHY BY ALI HARPER

ADDITIONAL PHOTOGRAPHY BY SARA LIGORRIA-TRAMP

CLARKSON POTTER/PUBLISHERS
NEW YORK

Published in the United States by Clarkson Potter/Publishers,
an imprint of Random House, a division of Penguin Random
House LLC, New York.
ClarksonPotter.com
RandomHouseBooks.com

CLARKSON POTTER is a trademark and POTTER
with colophon is a registered trademark of
Penguin Random House LLC.

Library of Congress Cataloging-in-Publication Data
is available upon request.

ISBN 978-0-593-23323-8
Ebook ISBN 978-0-593-23324-5

Printed in China

Photographers: Ali Harper and Sara Ligorria-Tramp
Editor: Angelin Borsics
Editorial Assistant: Darian Keels
Designer: Jennifer K. Beal Davis
Design Manager: Jen Wang
Production Editor: Terry Deal
Production Manager: Kim Tyner
Compositors: Merri Ann Morrell, Zoe Tokushige, and
Hannah Hunt
Copy Editor: Rachel Holzman
Marketer: Daniel Wikey
Publicist: Lauren Kretzschmar

10 9 8 7 6 5 4 3 2 1

First Edition

For my partner, Travis,
and my daughters,
Rachel, Emily, and
Natalie, who taught me
what home means

contents

WELCOME TO HOME THERAPY   9

the individual domain   18

the organizational domain   76

the communal domain   172

the renewal domain   242

RESOURCES   301
ACKNOWLEDGMENTS   302

welcome to home therapy

Hello. Come in, sit down, and get comfy. Congratulations on taking the first step toward creating a beautiful home that prioritizes your mental wellness. Maybe this isn't the first time you've opened a book about therapy, or perhaps you have no idea what therapy really is, and that's okay.

Therapy is for everyone. We all have challenges we face and could use someone to bounce ideas off of in order to navigate our way to the other side. And therapists are simply professionals who are there to help, by listening and offering solutions. Whether you are dealing with issues on your own or with a loved one, as a therapist-turned-interior-designer I have found the problems we face typically begin in the home—and they can be resolved in the home, too.

Consider placing a mirror on the opposite side of your favorite design feature in your home. This entry way mirror reflects beautifully the kitchen opposite this space.

Your Home,
Your Safe Space

You can't control what happens in the outside world, but at home you can find ways to feel renewed and fulfilled. While everyone's problems are wildly different, there are some fundamental similarities I often see. One of the most common issues stems from a failure to set boundaries. You might have trouble carving out time for your own creative enrichment in a busy household filled with children, or perhaps you have trouble going to bed on time and getting enough sleep. With proper boundaries in place, you can make more room for your personal enrichment and self-care.

Something else I frequently help others learn to do is to "live in the gray." Most people don't realize that they don't have to default to a black-and-white, either/or way of thinking. I remind them that sometimes you're happy and sometimes you're sad, and that's perfectly okay. (In fact, you can be happy and sad at the same time—it's an emotion called bittersweet.) Whether things work out or not, you have to remember that life circumstances can and often do change. The good news is that your home is the perfect place to experience and contain all of your emotions. And when you set up your home appropriately, you can process what you're feeling in the comforting cocoon of, say, a cozy chair surrounded by plants and calming colors, while you learn to live more comfortably with uncertainty. You don't have to let those feelings derail you because you know you're safe where you are. That is the promise of the Home Therapy method.

This leads me to a fundamental truth that is a big part of therapy: We are all born fragile and defenseless. But how we learn to deal with that vulnerability becomes the driving force of our lives. Most of us acknowledge that we come into the world vulnerable and leave it the same way; as a society, however, we somehow pretend that this shouldn't be true throughout the years we spend living our lives. Therapy acknowledges otherwise. Being vulnerable is important to establishing true connections with others, finding our authentic selves, and

When placing a sofa in front of a window, go for a low-back style, which allows for more light to flow into the space.

Match your undertones! The warmth in the wood credenza complements the brass details in the coffee table and picture frame.

feeling secure at home (insert home security pun!)—and, therefore, finding true happiness. But it's not easy to do, which is why having an environment in which to practice it fully is so important.

Home is the best place to form the ideas we carry with us into the world, so if we can learn to live in the world as we do at home, we can more confidently face our fears and show love to others. That's why I'm passionate not only about making your home a place where you are surrounded by elevated design, but also a place that elevates you as a human being.

As someone who has seen many kinds of family tragedy, navigated just about every design dilemma, and struggled with my own emotional growth, I want to share my experience on both a personal and professional level, and that's what we'll do in this book. We'll find out what weighs heavy on your mind and in your heart, and we'll lighten the load, because that's Home Therapy.

The Method

Before I became an interior designer, I worked as a licensed marriage and family therapist for seventeen years making house calls to those who needed my help. One of the things I noticed time and time again was that the home often reflected the issues through which we were working. After a while, I noticed that I could anticipate what the issues were going to be just by looking at the home. And in my practice, I saw it all. I worked with the most stressed-out, burned-out, and burdened populations among us. Couples who struggled with intimacy usually had piles of clothes on their beds, and families who felt as if their children were running their lives had toys, books, and shoes littering every surface.

Without realizing it, I started to develop the Home Therapy Method. Slowly but surely, I pinpointed four necessary "domains" that one had to become aware of to improve his or her quality of life in the modern world. These domains are common in all homes, and all families, around the world. They are simply part of being human. You can set them up as simple layers or areas in every room of the home to 1. help you establish a strong identity, 2. establish clear organization of your things, 3. connect with others in your home, and 4. practice your own self-care.

Once all four domains are addressed in the home, you'll see your self-esteem soar, your relationships grow, your days become easier, and your spirit lighten.

1. THE INDIVIDUAL DOMAIN

Before you start designing your home, it's important to get to know your authentic self. So we begin with a look inward. Ultimately, this domain is an exploration of your hopes, dreams, vulnerabilities, strengths, and weaknesses. We will work from the inside out, mining that rich well of your soul to find your cornerstone and set aside space specifically to help you accomplish your goals. You'll identify your Core Desire, or what motivates you, which will inform how you approach all the other domains/parts of my method. Everything you learn in part one forms the foundation for the rest of your Home Therapy journey.

2. THE ORGANIZATIONAL DOMAIN

In order to be successful in the world, we need to feel safe and secure. The organizational domain helps you do just that by emphasizing containment and routine so that you feel soothed by an internal structure. Even if you're not a minimalist, by making your home highly functional, you'll gain confidence and feel even more efficient when you step outside your home.

3. THE COMMUNAL DOMAIN

Home is where our most intimate moments take place, and it sets us up for how we communicate with the world. That's why this domain is about forming more authentic connections with those who live in or visit your home. Here we will discuss utilizing good design layout to allow for cherished bonding time—along with sharing entertaining tips and fun decorating ideas. In this part, we will also focus on practicing greater listening and empathy skills for more honest and successful communication.

4. THE RENEWAL DOMAIN

This domain is about creating the right energy and environment for your personal rejuvenation, because everyone needs time to recharge. Using sound and light therapy, crystals, bath rituals, weighted blankets, white space, and more, this domain focuses on self-care to revitalize the mind, body, and spirit systems. This is where you find time to enjoy the fruits of your labor from the other domains, and just relax.

How to Use This Book 🧰

I imagine this book as a toolbox. Maybe it's an old, rusty gunmetal one sitting in a shed in your backyard that I help you to dust off and teach you to use its contents with renewed vigor, or maybe it's a brand-new, sleek and modern colorful box you're looking to open for the first time. Either way, this toolbox will have the capacity to transform the way you live. As both a therapist and a consummate DIY-er, this is a metaphor I'm constantly thinking about and exploring.

As you turn the pages, I'll be picturing you diving into your trusty kit filled with both sturdy hammers and sharp

nails—or, in this case, essential life skills like better organizational habits and clear communication. The goal is for you to be able to reach for these tools any time and feel as if your dream home (and life) is at your fingertips.

In each part of the book I'll ask that you take stock and ask yourself certain questions that a therapist would pose to you. Then, just as if I were your personal $300-an-hour therapist, I will give you specific tools 🧰 to change your habits, shift your mindset, and become more in touch with your thoughts and feelings.

For those who learn best by example, throughout the book you'll find beautiful examples of good design along with accessible tips. I asked those who participated in this project and opened their homes to me to also open their hearts and minds, and the transformations were

breathtaking. I'll take you from an art studio in Atlanta to a writer's den in New York City to a mother of three's kitchen in California. Those featured in the book filled out the same questionnaire that I will ask you to fill out (see page 16), and you will see how they transformed their beliefs within the four walls of their homes.

Finally, this book is designed to be used for life. It is a handbook and will mean something different to you each time you open it and refresh your relationship with the method. As your relationship with yourself and with those around you evolves, you will likely find new things to explore in this book.

If you show up for the method and do the work, it will show up for you. So let's get started. Open your bountiful, beautiful toolbox and let's start building something incredible.

The Intake Form

Now that you know the method, it's time to dig a little deeper into what's going on in your home. I want you to connect with the larger picture of your physical home space as well as understand your mental home space. As with any new therapy or design client, I accomplish that through what we call an Intake Form. Here I ask a series of questions about your home, your emotional well-being, your family history, your aesthetic preferences, and the state of your current relationships.

Please take the time for yourself to fill out the Intake Form! It might look a bit daunting, but once you start to become an observer of your own life, doors will open and you won't want them to shut.

After you have completed your Intake Form, play therapist (yes, you!) and pretend you are someone else reading this form. What would you think about this person's home? What would you pinpoint as their main issues? What do you think they would need to feel confident and happy in their space? How would you describe their style? Read through every response and start gathering information. The fog will start lifting a bit and you can begin to see why certain spaces aren't reaching their full potential. Later you'll learn how to actually design your home. For now, your job is to start playing detective and look for clues about your best home and life.

To download and print the Intake Form, open the camera app on your phone, place the QR code above within view, and click the link that pops up.

DEFINING YOUR CORE DESIRE

Reflect on your answers from your Intake Form. What did you learn about yourself and your home? As you move through this book, you'll gain plenty of inspiration—whether colors, patterns, new furniture arrangements, or other details—to help you decorate your home. But before you begin, you'll want to start making connections between your Intake Form and your overall vision for your home design, so your design is backed by intention. We call this your Core Desire and discovering your Core Design is key to the Home Therapy Method.

To define your Core Design, ask yourself the following questions:

- What rooms in your house are working for you and bring you joy? How do they elevate your goals, strengthen relationships, keep you structured and organized, or help you rejuvenate?
- What parts of your house or rooms elicit negative feelings? How are they detrimental to your goals, relationships, structure, or relaxation? What feelings do you wish you felt instead in these spaces?
- Why do you want these things to change?

Keep asking *why* a few more times. That is your **CORE DESIRE**. Connect to it.

Now reflect on what change you can bring about:

- Name three things you can do to update this space (hint: pick a new wall color, add lighting, or switch up the room layout).
- Imagine a scenario where these problems are solved. Close your eyes and visualize the room in that new way. How do you feel?
- How do you want to feel overall when you step into your home? Why?

Congrats! You just learned visualization to connect to your Core Desire. This is your road map for this book. Let's begin.

the individual domain

If you don't form a solid identity at home, you risk letting the world define you. That's why we begin the Home Therapy method by addressing the Individual Domain: Each room in your house can help you understand yourself and achieve your greater purpose in life.

In part 1, we're going to dig deep, like back-of-the-junk-drawer deep. Because once you become curious about yourself and your inner world, you will begin to see the link between your own mental wellness and how your space is set up. From there, it becomes much easier to make changes to your physical surroundings. You might think you know all there is to know about yourself, but until you sit down and really consider your life goals and the beliefs that could be holding you back, you might not realize your potential for change. Personal spaces can be incredible tools that we use to build up those definitions

and connect to our motivations without facing fear of comparison or the judgment of others. Our goal in this section is to strengthen your unshakable sense of self and to enable you to design a few places in your home that will embolden that realized self so that you can face anything the outside world throws at you.

We fill our homes with beliefs that frame what we think is and isn't possible, and that are likely holding us back in unexplored ways. Your home should not only be a beautiful reflection of your personal style, but it should also give you solace and space to allow your dreams to grow—whether you want to become a confident home cook or finally write that novel. Once you free your mind from any limiting ideas you have about yourself or your family, you can create new beliefs and make your home a place of limitless potential. I can't wait to show you how.

PREVIOUS PAGE: These sheer curtain panels add a soft texture to the space, and their neutral color helps keep the focus on the gorgeous armchairs.

OPPOSITE: Natural light is the best way to make a space feel open. Allow your windows to be a design statement on their own.

get on the positive loop

My friend Rachel lives alone and her mother is widowed, so she thought it might be a good idea for the two of them to get an app that allows them to track each other's phones as a safety measure. At first this was a novelty. *I see you're at the gym!* her mother would text. *I see you're home!* Rachel would write back. Yet after a while, the fun wore off as they realized they each went to the same places every day: work, gym, home, restaurant, home. On weekends they frequented the same brunch spots. Her mother golfed every Sunday. Rachel hosted dinner parties every Friday. When they saw each other for lunch, Rachel asked her mother, "Are you still liking the app?"

"Sure, it works great," her mother said, "but we're not very interesting. We're both just on a loop." Up until then, they'd thought they were engaging in a wide variety of activities, but Rachel's mom was right: They were drawing circles on a map—just as many of us follow a pretty regular routine. While some might be an exception—those who travel frequently for work, for example—we still have our rituals no matter where we are, whether those loops are useful or not. The common denominator for us all is that we usually start out, and end up, at home.

We are also on loops within our homes.

Tucking your microwave behind a pantry door is a convenience that helps encourage you to cook fresh meals.

Unpacking Your Home Loop

Along these routes in our homes, we experience all kinds of signals that stimulate the rote, reptilian parts of our brains to perform certain tasks. Whether it's an alarm clock waking us in the morning, or the end of a TV show telling us it's time to get a snack (or five), our homes teach us to do the same activities and even think the same things over and over. It can become a little like living in a trance if we don't challenge our reality and try to break the spell from time to time.

Have you ever wondered why certain people can do exceptional things—like run a marathon? Well, I'm here to tell you that those people are no different than you; they just might be on a more intentional loop. When you establish a good loop in your home, tasks that help you get fit or increase productivity become less of a "fight" and more of a habit—like brushing your teeth before bed. Positive loops can create new grooves in your brain so that tasks that serve your goals send good signals to your brain and thus become more enjoyable—or at least easier. The key is to switch up your old grooves, but in order to change, you need to design your home to accommodate the new loops you're creating.

Say your goal is to exercise in the morning. The first day, maybe you wake up a little late, tired from a poor night's sleep, and you think you've missed your chance. Plus, your equipment is all the way in the basement—out of sight. So you don't work

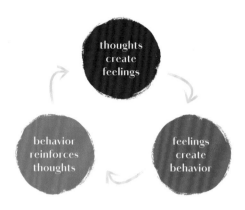

out, which confirms to your brain that you did not have that extra time anyway (just look at all the other things you had to do!), and then your mind relaxes. You avoided the hard work of exercise. The signal you've sent your brain is momentary pleasure because you got to stay sedentary. Phew, no new grooves created!

Now imagine that you designed an Individual Domain in your bedroom that supports your exercise goal. You wake up, grab your journal off your nightstand, sit in a comfortable chair, and write two pages to dispel any negative thoughts. You're ready to test the idea that you have ten minutes to work out *no matter what.* You don't really want to exercise, but you see your yoga mat, Habit Board, and pretty Intention Tray (we'll get to those later), all of which send signals to your brain that everything is ready to go—your workout is possible. *You can do this!* You work out for

OPPOSITE: The items you keep on your nightstand can help underscore your home loop. Here, a place to set jewelry, a teacup, and some aromatherapy encourages better sleep.

ten minutes and feel great. Then you add a mark to your Habit Board. Voilà! New groove city.

Eventually your workouts make you feel so good that you begin increasing them to twenty and thirty minutes a day. Your rational, truth-seeking brain now has proof—it trusts in this and gets on board. You've altered your old reality, and you've changed your beliefs about who you are as a person. Even if you miss a day here or there, you'll look forward to getting back into the new groove as soon as possible.

So what's the big takeaway here? If you can just revise your loop by designing a few Individual Domains in your home, nothing can stop you! But how do you do that? Try coming up with some physical cues that will send the right signals to your brain. Let's explore how.

ABOVE: It's easy to put those takeout menus away when bowls, plates, and cooking utensils are ready to be put to use.

OPPOSITE: Keeping your workout items in view is a great way to remind yourself to maintain healthy self-care habits.

SPOTLIGHT
Clever Coffee Bar

Positive loops that help you eat heathier start with great planning. This stylish coffee and tea bar is the brainchild of a beverage-loving homeowner. To encourage herself to plan healthy meals for the week, she created an Individual Domain—a seating area—right by her beverage station. Because the space is inviting, she is motivated to sit here and write out meal plans while referencing her cookbooks and staying hydrated. The beauty of the station—and the stylish gold SodaStream—pull her toward this part of the kitchen to take breaks throughout the day. She's also included various crystals, which help her draw the energy she needs—specifically strength, motivation, clarity, and love. With her coffee and tea each morning, this practice sets her up on a strong and beautiful positive loop for the day and week ahead!

ABOVE: Play with your Intention Tray! Layer texture, color, and varied materials to make it yours.

DESIGN TIPS

1. Go for purposeful contrast to add visual interest—thick and thin, delicate and heavy, open and solid.

2. Remind yourself to keep your chin up by making the most of vertical space with shelves, hooks, art, and hanging plants.

3. Decide whether you want calm colors to soothe you or vibrant colors to energize you—and make sure those colors connect you to your purpose.

⚒ THE INTENTION TRAY

We humans are visual creatures and sometimes need reminders to stay on our positive loop. Visualization is a powerful tool. Many studies have shown that if you can imagine yourself doing something, you can actually improve at that task. Athletes do this in their practice. Designers do this with mood boards. You can do it at home. Enter Intention Trays! These compact design moments showcase specific items on a tray to remind you of your purpose and help you stay on track with your goals. They're a handy tool I developed as part of my method that anyone can pull together. Best of all, they look great in any room. And no one but you needs to know what your Intention Tray is for!

We're bombarded with images on television and social media that don't always serve us, but your home is one environment that you can control. These trays are an empowering way to harness your own space and make it a place that serves your goals and needs.

Using a tray with a neutral finish will help your accessories and fresh flowers pop.

HOW TO STYLE AN INTENTION TRAY

The reason real estate agents style or stage a house is because they're trying to set up a kind of "movie" for you while you're walking through the home. They want you to visualize the stories (hopefully starring you!) that can play out in every room. In the same way, Intention Trays are all about the story you want to tell about yourself, your home, and, well, your intentions. You can design more than one Intention Tray (for more than one intention you might have!) and position them in different areas of your home for helpful reminders and to establish new loops. Here's how to create them:

1. **Decide what your intention is.** Start writing down your intentions in a special journal and pick one intention that is the most significant for you.

2. **Find a tray and a space to put it.** Trays are useful intention tools because they're simple containers that can hold your story—by literally presenting it to you on a tray—plus, they look pretty on any surface. Ideally, you'll place your tray wherever you can sit and focus on yourself and that specific goal. Just make sure that the tray works in both shape and scale for where you want to place it (keeping in mind that other people in your family might need to use this surface, too).

3. **Choose your objects and style them!** Mixing colors and materials is a way to keep your décor visually interesting. You can either use hues from the opposite sides of the color wheel to make them pop (think navy and coral) or you can pick a single color and create a softer story. Consider your surface, too: If you have a light-colored coffee table, choose at least one or two darker objects and vice versa. Gather a variety of objects: small, medium, large, and round, square, and oval.

4. **Think three's company.** Style three objects (or groupings of smaller items) together as one winning number. I say "groupings" because a stack of books with large wooden beads on top would count as one unit. No need to get technical about this. If it looks good to your eye, then it's perfect.

5. **Don't overlook the less obvious places.** Coffee and dining tables will likely already have décor, but Intention Trays are also important on dressers, desks, bathroom counters, entryway consoles, and in workout rooms and creative spaces.

SPOTLIGHT
Artist's Intention Tray

The plant here isn't just for the fresh air and the calming signals greenery sends to our brains; it also serves as natural inspiration for this artist's work. She even incorporates the leaves into her sculptures. It's a reminder of her intentions to connect with nature, too. Notice the quote, which is attributed to her favorite artist, Pablo Picasso: *"Art washes away from the soul the dust of everyday life."*

"ART WASHES AWAY FROM THE SOUL
THE DUST OF EVERYDAY LIFE"
-PABLO PICASSO

unearth your limiting beliefs

While visual signals are an important part of establishing a more positive loop, believing you are a person who can and will follow through on completing your loop is key. We all attach limiting beliefs to our homes, which could be holding us back from ultimately achieving our goals.

Also known as cognitive distortions, limiting beliefs are the things we wish we could be or do but that don't seem possible. These ideas are formed while we're young and follow us into adulthood, even though they're not really true and don't serve us well. They can seem very real, and many people embrace them thinking they're being "realistic." We often glean these false beliefs from experiences we've had, most likely within our homes, providing what we think is evidence about our own limitations.

When we tell ourselves we're not good enough or deserving of something, we miss out on reaching our full potential. We might hold back for fear of failing, or we may keep from expanding our social circles for fear of judgment. But we can free ourselves! The antidote to limiting beliefs is to uncover and "truth test" them so that we can provide new evidence to contradict our old identities. If we use our homes to aid us in this work, and to empower and uplift us, then we can find peace and move forward. First, we need to bring these thoughts into the light and challenge them, and then we can see that they don't have to be our stories.

Surrounding yourself with things that bring you joy—a musical instrument, pretty plants, and a cozy blanket—helps you combat any limiting beliefs you might have about yourself.

Confronting My Own Limiting Beliefs

Growing up, I had the good fortune of learning from strong female role models. My maternal grandfather died young of tuberculosis, leaving my grandmother widowed with four children during wartime. As a single mom, she needed to earn a living on her own, so she opened a general store while teaching herself about importing goods. She even learned Russian. Then, in 1943 when my family had to flee Shanghai and leave everything behind, my grandmother started all over again in Taiwan. This time she opened a bakery and an import/export store in Taipei, which still runs today. Because of her experience, she raised her children to be survivors—to be strong, proud, and practical just as she was.

In her early twenties, my mother emigrated from Taipei to the United States for a better life. She was sent on a graduate exchange program and spoke very little English. She ended up in Kansas City, Missouri, and it might as well have been another planet! As an Asian woman in an all-white world, she struggled to assimilate, pushing through and eventually receiving a master's degree in microbiology. She pivoted and ended up carving out a successful career as a real estate broker and raised two girls while juggling everything, all at once, all the time.

While my mother and grandmother set great examples of hard work and survival, the challenges they faced also taught them to be practical. They believed pragmatism was what kept you afloat, and, while they were both creatives at heart who loved making elaborate home décor and crafts, the idea of producing art as a livelihood was not acceptable to them. That was a recipe for disaster.

Enter my limiting beliefs.

Many people might not know it from my sunny, can-do attitude, but I fought my limiting beliefs for a long time and still need what I call "tune-ups" to keep my depression and anxiety at bay. It wasn't until I started seeing a therapist that I realized how entrenched I was with my old identity and past home experiences.

The first step to my recovery was unearthing my restricting thoughts so that I could confront them and stop them in their tracks. I believed that interior design could never be a "real" career and that anything a person loved to do wasn't a practical way to make money. As the child of immigrants, I also thought that anything I did had to be perfect. I alone was responsible for embodying the American dream. I mean, those are some big shoes to fill! But I managed to reteach myself that those thoughts didn't have to be my story, and I did it with the help of my home.

Limiting beliefs can be inherited from those who love you the most and are the most well meaning. You likely admire and respect those who handed you these beliefs, so you assume they must be right. There are also the ideas you've learned from those naysayers who put you down in the past. It might be natural to think these negative nellies are "truth tellers" while everyone else is just being polite. You can also form limiting beliefs on your own by comparing yourself to others. Maybe you can think of a time when you didn't feel you measured up and, instead, you let others define what is "good" and "bad." Um, hello social media! There's photographic evidence that others are doing better than you are, right? Yeah, not so much.

How I Reframed My Story

Unhelpful thoughts about my home paralyzed me for almost a decade. Even after living there for ten years, I hadn't hung a single painting! Then I went to therapy. I realized that I was afraid to ruin everything. I had to learn that nothing was permanent. Oh, and I was also terrified to admit to anyone my dream of becoming an interior designer.

I fought my perfectionism and doubts, reminded myself that everything can be fixed, and finally picked up a hammer and nail and hung a picture. Then I kept going. I made tons of mistakes. But I fixed them. I learned that it is within my power to repair things I "mess up," and that mistakes aren't a big deal. Plus, I acquired all this knowledge about myself from the safe cocoon of my home with no one watching or judging me. The only person I had to prove anything to was myself. Soon I was surrounded by family photos and inspiring quotes and images, and I finally felt free.

Here are the thoughts that broke me out of my limiting beliefs:

- Making mistakes does not mean I want or can't be an amazing designer.

- What's the big deal if I put a hole in the wall? If I decide it's in the wrong spot, I can always learn to patch it up.

I saw how automatic it was for me, and eventually for my clients, to bring old thought patterns into new homes. But once I took ownership of my surroundings, my pride and belief in what was possible grew, too. I began to own my identity at home and challenged my story, which allowed me to change the narrative. Soon after, I finally felt authentic. My thought pattern changed from limited to unlimited.

By reframing my story,
I was able to start a
career as an interior
designer, and now I
have a beautiful kitchen
to show for it!

What's Holding You Back?

Let's explore some notions you have about yourself by looking at a few common core limiting beliefs. Remember, these are subconscious thoughts, so while they may sound a bit direct on the surface, I implore you to dig deep to see if any resonate with you. As you think about the types of limiting beliefs you might hold, brainstorm ways you can use the spaces of your home to help you combat those untruths.

Automatic negative thoughts (ANTs), or belief blockers as I call them, make life difficult: They can stall your decision-making, lower your self-esteem, strain your relationships, and lead to depression, anxiety, and even anger. They're what fuel your core limiting beliefs, and it's important for you to identify and call them out so you can take away their power and regain control over your thoughts, moods, and behaviors. Here are a few examples:

• Fortunetelling: This is the belief blocker of almost anyone who has a panic disorder. These beliefs are masterful at predicting the worst-case scenario, even though they don't have any evidence. When you find yourself imagining the worst possible outcome, pause and question the assumptions behind it. Are there equally likely, more positive outcomes that you're overlooking?

• Guilt-tripping: These beliefs involve words like *should*, *must*, *ought*, and *have*

to. Words we use to talk to ourselves are very important. Guilt is not a very good motivator for change. Telling yourself *I should go see my grandmother* only serves to make you feel negative. Instead, flip the script: *My grandmother will be so happy to see me.*

• Blaming: Whenever you blame someone else for the problems in your life, you victimize yourself and prevent yourself from doing anything to change it. Many of us play the blame game, but it rarely helps us. Stay away from blaming thoughts and take personal responsibility for changing the problems you can control.

• Labeling: Calling yourself or someone else a derogatory name diminishes your ability to see situations clearly. Plus, labels are very harmful. Stay away from them.

Whenever you find yourself feeling mad, sad, nervous, or out of control, head to one of your designated Individual Domains and write down in your journal what you are thinking. Identify which belief blocker is infesting your mind, then tell it to leave your house and never come back! In the following pages, I'll help you with techniques you can use at home to do just that.

CLOCKWISE FROM TOP LEFT: Outfit your home in small but mighty ways to break those irksome limiting beliefs! Try putting a ZZ plant in a soothing-colored planter on your desk. • Hang shelves filled with art brushes, paints, and colored pencils nearby for a quick sketch to let out your stress. • A bedside acrylic box with a small notepad and pencil is easy to access when your thoughts keep you tossing and turning at night.

Flipping the Script

Limiting beliefs can come at us from many angles. But no matter what the limiting belief, you can flip the script! Use this process as a jumping-off point for exploring your own thoughts:

1. Consider what you think a home should be. How have the homes you've lived in measured up against this ideal?

2. Ask yourself what your triggers are. What makes you feel unsure or unsafe? How do you generally deal with those feelings at home?

3. Go on a field trip around your home. What limiting beliefs do you have in each room? Does the kitchen conjure guilty thoughts of not cooking enough? Does the dining room remind you of challenging family dynamics? Don't judge yourself for having these thoughts. Instead, just be curious and gather information. Which rooms make you feel happy and warm? Why? What is the décor like in there?

4. Explore the stories that made you believe in these untruths. Where did this "evidence" come from? Test reality by becoming skeptical of these limiting stories.

5. Start challenging these beliefs and the stories from which they originated. What assumptions are you making?

6. Now flip the script. Start writing down equally believable alternatives to these stories that you can start to get behind.

Before we can change things, we need to know what we're up against. Spoiler alert: You may not believe these new stories yet, but that's okay. Your old identity won't fall away overnight. It will take time and practice and the help of tools such as your Intention Trays, your Habit Boards, and other positive loops you reinforce through your home design.

ABOVE: A round tray on a square is a subtle way of playing with different shapes. The glass and brass framing lend ethereal yet organized storage for the bedside.

OPPOSITE: Hanging a light gives you more surface space on your nightstand.

create a place of pause

Now that we're working on a new story, let's take a minute. By this point in part 1, you've had a lot of information to process. Give yourself a moment to put the book down, close your eyes, and take a deep breath in through your nose for three seconds and out through your mouth for eight seconds. Then open your eyes and come back to this page.

Feel better? I hope so. It's important to practice pausing because, honestly, it's hard to shift any mindset. Living in the present is an acquired skill. While it might seem like a simple concept, it's a major challenge without (and even with!) a space to practice these tools. And while many of us have "spots" in our homes that we call ours, like an office or a walk-in closet, most of us don't have enough. Pausing is one of the most important, transformative, and underrated tools we have in our toolbox, and the spaces that invite you to take a minute, regroup, reframe, and contemplate should be readily available any time you need them. They can be spots where you give yourself a quick time-out to breathe deeply, or places where you can enjoy "me time." Consider a cozy chair by a window with a chic side table that holds a leather-bound thought journal, a window seat in the hallway, or a reading nook in the living room. The main requirement is that this space is always accessible, and just for use by one person at a time.

Using warm wood tones paired with black hexagonal-tiled flooring in your bathroom creates a cozy, comforting yet bold look.

Once you design a solo spot full of warmth and comfort, you can take a step back and reframe your thoughts. That doesn't mean you're going to feel instantly positive and peaceful. Our homes symbolize so much. They are the physical structures we create for ourselves and a holding container in which we live with the good, the bad, and the uncertain. Everything is a balancing act. Giving yourself a moment to pause, to experience that ambivalence, and to embrace the imperfection and discomfort is an essential step in the journey.

Here in your pause place you can practice being okay "messing up" and not being perfect. You can accept yourself and make a new plan for next time when something goes wrong—preferably with your journal! I call this the emotional

ecosystem, where you can just be with what is at present and make peace with it. This is a space where the lows and highs can coexist. A healthy environment prioritizes the expression of both—and they need one another in order to create depth in our lives. Think yin and yang.

It might sound like I'm asking you to keep your emotions inside, but it's quite the opposite. The key to framing your feelings is letting those waves of emotion break over you but not carry you away. That happens when you create a cozy cocoon where all of these emotions can live with you in comfort and harmony. Your body, your finances, your relationships, or your home might not be in the shape you wish they were, and that's okay. Nothing is permanent. All of this will change, and the good news is that you have the power to change it.

Bright Bedroom Nook

This homeowner knows what it's like to hold the good and the bad in one space. An anesthesiologist and mother of two sons, she and her husband experienced a long and arduous process building their home. After working on their new construction for a full year and then parting ways with their initial contractor, they embarked on the emotionally taxing journey of stripping their home down to the studs and restarting from scratch. She and her husband even went to couples' therapy to tackle the stress of the rebuild, but now they appreciate every nook and cranny of the home even more. As part of their journey, this homeowner was tasked with accepting her space as a container for her feelings, from frustration to joy. She even uses this reading nook in her bedroom for her virtual therapy sessions that are focused on her weekly growth. Here she can process all of her feelings before moving through her day.

In its own quiet way, this Individual Domain captures my Home Therapy method perfectly. Not only does it make use of an otherwise underused corner space, it also plays with shape, color, and texture in the most organic way. With a muted palette, you get the most out of the colors by juxtaposing complementary hues, like the orange and blue here. Because these colors sit opposite each other on the color wheel, they draw each other out. The layers of texture throughout help make the space exciting enough to call the owner back to this room, but calming enough for her to unwind and find herself.

She also chose a space with natural light to inspire maximum reflection and stillness. She can sit here at any time of the day and pause to help her live a more connected and centered life. Not bad for one little bedroom nook, right?

DESIGN TIPS

1. Use black paint or metal to make elements in a room pop without being too bold—like the fireplace and windows here.

2. Choose furniture that accentuates the space. A tall wingback chair in this corner elongates the nook and makes this ordinary corner look custom designed.

3. Make sure you sit in a variety of seat depths and know your sweet spot for comfort. The ideal seat depth for a lounge chair is generally 15 to 18 inches.

This corner was very tall indeed. Play with the idea of using a tall tree to add vertical interest instead of more artwork. Now the homeowner has a visual break in a space where she can safely surrender her thoughts.

SPOTLIGHT
A Teenager's Hideaway

This client created a hideaway for her seventeen-year-old son to seek refuge while he wrestles with teenage emotions. A hideaway is especially useful for teens who crave independence but still need structure and guidance. Here he draws and sketches out his feelings in the form of dragons and medieval times, which are his hobby and passion. His favorite pet—a bearded dragon—lives here as well. His Intention Tray reflects his passions with a dragonhead figurine, a sketchbook, and a special rock collection. Without the Home Therapy method this space might have become a closet or a workspace, but instead it shows how we can rethink all of the spaces in our homes so they can nurture and elevate us in unexpected ways.

This space is a great example of mixed and matched textiles and shapes. Each pillow is a different size, texture, and design but the color palette is limited, which pulls it all together. The rugs can also function as great throws! The jute rug over the daybed is a perfect accent for this space. The bookshelf door allows for extra storage and is a fun reminder that this leads to the teen's own private, magical world.

In the bedroom, the sconces are a space-saving and attractive way to flank each side of the bed. The dark metal lends a moody and masculine flair to the room while the wood and plant life soften the look. Plus, nightstands are a wonderful opportunity to display journals, plants, and crystals, so the more surface area, the better!

DESIGN TIPS

1. Always ask for your children's input and implement realistic ideas. If they know they are heard, they'll likely trust you more. Yay for trust!

2. Teens can be messy, so consider using sturdy materials, like metal baskets instead of fabric-lined ones and stain-resistant fabrics for pillows and seating.

3. Let them choose their art. This is a fun way for them to learn how to express themselves—even if it isn't your taste. Hello, dragons!

4. All teens need incentives, especially when it comes to studying. Make their desk area an inviting place with a modern, comfortable chair and a cool, soft-glowing lamp.

5. Novelty lighting such as neon signs or LED accent lighting around the ceiling's perimeter is a whimsical way to illuminate their bedrooms and keep things interesting!

6. If your teen wants to change up the décor, go for new bedding, which is an economical way to refresh a room. Bold geometric shapes, ocean waves, boho dreamy plants—so many possibilities to channel your teen's vibe.

SPOTLIGHT
A Writer's Retreat

This client is a busy writer who juggles clients and her own business, so a reading corner offers her a respite. For her, living in New York City can feel overwhelming, and when she quiets her mind, she finds it fills up with to-do lists at warp speed. Even though her living room is small, she was very intentional about creating a moment for herself that is readily accessible and comfortable. Here she tests her limiting beliefs and proves they are not real by listing out accomplishments. It's also the place she comes to reconnect with big-picture goals. She positioned the spot in full view of New York City so she can enjoy the skyline while reflecting and jotting down notes.

ABOVE: Small patterned trays pack a big statement punch to help you manifest your wildest dreams.

BELOW: Don't underestimate those window sills! Most sills are just wide enough to accommodate your favorite books or a small potted plant.

OPPOSITE: If your furniture isn't large enough to fill the room, an area rug will help do the trick!

DESIGN TIPS

1. Choose décor that supports your Core Desire. Here, floating shelves stacked with books and literary art reaffirm this homeowner's identity as a writer.

2. Add beauty to functional spaces. A pretty patterned rug and a showstopper pendant put this writer in the right mindset for working long hours.

3. In a small space, get creative with office chairs. Rather than dark wood furniture, which might clutter the room visually, we chose lighter tones, including an acrylic chair (that's surprisingly comfortable!).

gain a new perspective

I love, love, love to move things around. Maybe it's the Aries in me, but changing around furniture and moving art from one wall to another is my design jam. You will be amazed at how switching up the flow of your space can mentally change your attitude. To start, find a new spot in your room where you can gain a new perspective. Consider the story your home is telling by asking yourself these questions. (Note: There are no right or wrong answers, and "I don't know" is fine, too!)

1. In three words, describe the home of the person you wish to be. What steps, if any, can you take to align your home with that home?

2. How can I honor my home and thank it for all that it does for me? List three home repairs needed, and create an action plan for getting them done.

3. What would I think of my home if I saw it for the first time? List two easy ways to improve your home if it doesn't currently suit you.

4. Can I create something magical with an unused corner?

Patterned furniture can be tamed by layering neutral pillows or throws. The space-saving chair design makes it easy to move around the room for a change in scenery.

ABOVE: A vintage dresser adds great character and organization—the ideal spot for this stylist's Intention Tray.

RIGHT: For better sleep, consider investing in flax linen bed sheets. They prevent you from overheating at night and breathe with you in warmer seasons.

OPPOSITE: This mid-century modern valet chair was designed so that men could hang their jacket on the back and store a shoe brush on top. A perfect statement piece for this stylist's room!

soothe yourself

Okay, so this is a biggie. Self-soothing is something we're theoretically supposed to learn as babies (yes, babies!), but it's a tougher concept to implement than you might think. While pausing allows us space to plan our next moves and regroup, we all need something a little different during high-stress times. Self-soothing rebalances our emotional ecosystems. Often, our emotions want to overtake our rational brains and steer the ship. The key to reigning in these feelings, and staying on the positive loop, is to self-soothe. But in our search for security, we may end up looking for love in all the wrong places. That could include numbing ourselves with television, emotional eating, or a bottle of wine.

Once in a while these practices are okay—you're only human!—but putting them in your regular loop doesn't serve you. By becoming aware of the need to self-soothe and of what your coping mechanisms are, you can change your habits. And you have the best chance of success in implementing the new, healthy habits if you set up these practices at home. Write down a list of ten comforting actions you can take and place it in one of your pause spots. Here are some ideas: go for a long walk, water and talk to your plants, light a candle, call a friend, ask for a hug. (Combine a few of these to amp up the soothing factor!) Make the first item on your list something you can do right there in your window seat or kitchen chair and come back to it when you're tempted to stay in an unhelpful loop activity.

A morning cup of coffee enjoyed in a comfy chair by a bright window increases serotonin, which plays a role in regulating mood, emotions, appetite, and digestion.

Mixing wood tones in a space works when the undertones are similar. Here, the warm undertones provide continuity and calm.

INSTALLING A SOOTHING SWING

This swing chair is a great example of a soothing spot. Between the curved back of the chair acting as a cocoon and the lush plant life, it is set up to lull us into a calmer state. The space invites one to surrender to the gentle rocking of the chair and the fragrance coming from the plants. Add music or aromatherapy to the scene, close your eyes, and let your mind run free until your thoughts slow to a lumber. This is a great place to practice any of our soothing techniques like sipping a cup of tea or reaching out to a friend.

A hanging chair is a win for small corners or open spaces that need seating; it organically defines a sitting area vertically when a regular chair won't fit. Adding a side table not only makes it comfy, but also further defines the space. A swing by the fireside is an unconventional way to add seating and create a connecting moment to yourself. This is super DIYable with ceiling hooks, rope, and a wooden plank the size of a seat.

DESIGN TIPS

1. If you don't have a swinging chair, swivel chairs, rocking chairs, and even gliders are excellent alternatives for the gentle back-and-forth or side-to-side motion that soothes us.

2. Once your hanging chair is in place, test it out to see if you need to add cushioning. You can make an envelope pillow (no zippers needed) or use a 20-by-20-inch pillow as a seat cushion.

3. Sensory chairs, which are swing chairs made of one large swath of fabric, are easy to DIY with chic colorful canvas or a drop cloth. Be sure to use large wooden dowels and sturdy eye hooks.

Rugs are great for anchoring a space. If you want to designate a room for a certain purpose without adding walls, throw in an area rug.

practice
accountability

Now that you're becoming more self-aware in your space, you'll learn to trust yourself, and your home, more. Whether that means being okay with accidentally burning dinner, making bad art, or standing in front of the mirror buck naked and accepting your body, trust is key in allowing your home to help you. The confidence you get from knowing and trusting yourself will also help you set boundaries.

I'm sure you've heard about setting boundaries with other people (we'll cover that in the Communal Domain, page 172), but here we're talking about setting up boundaries with yourself. That means things you will and won't do, such as foods you will and won't bring into your home or the rules you establish surrounding the use of electronics before bedtime. The more you study your own habits, the easier it will be to know which boundaries to make for yourself. Here is my own home boundary list. You can make one, too.

Unique serving utensils can help elevate your at-home dining experience.

MY PERSONAL BOUNDARY LIST

1. Devices go back to charging stations at night and my kids earn their time for the next day.

2. I do NOT look at social media or emails as soon as I wake up. That time is juicy and ripe for an authentic moment to better myself, so I choose to meditate or work out. Or just enjoy a cup of joe before the kids wake up!

3. The kitchen is closed after dinner. I do not step foot in it because I will likely want to snack. (Nighttime eating is my kryptonite habit!)

4. Every item has a home and it must go back to it immediately. I cannot let things accumulate. If I see a stray pair of scissors, I make it a point to walk upstairs and put it back in the drawer. Even if it's a hassle, I just do it.

5. I think of working out as another habit like brushing my teeth. I'm not perfect but I set myself up to remember to do it by including a workout corner in the bathroom. No excuses if my workout clothes are literally next to my toothbrush!

Establishing a Creative Flow

Let's get weird! Yup, I'm talking about setting up a creative area, where you will expend and expel creative energy, which, when left unattended, can be harmful to the soul. Even if you don't think of yourself as an "artsy" type, creation is still part of human nature. A flow space can be anything from an easel and paints set up in the corner of a room to a piano corner. It simply needs to be a space in which you release tension in a positive way with no agenda. Think craft room, dance floor, tumbling mat, gardening shed, drum set, or baking corner. This isn't about pausing or relaxing, it's about spending excess energy. And before you assume your drum set is going to disturb the entire household, set aside those limiting beliefs and start questioning what's actually possible. (It's not that hard to soundproof a room, so rock on.) Here is a great place to look at your home, and your dreams, in a new way so that you always have space for your own fulfillment. Pick your no-screen creative outlet and write it down. Name three ways you can make it happen along with a realistic timeline for pursuing it.

ABOVE: These large folding doors were a big investment, but they were important to this homeowner for allowing fresh air into her at-home yoga studio.

OPPOSITE: Get creative with your end tables! Using items you already have is always a money-saver.

An Artist's Retreat

This ceramic artist lives with her husband and two children in a wellness community outside Atlanta, Georgia. The studio in her home is solely dedicated to her creativity and soul-searching. Her mantra is "Art is impatient meditation." She believes the process itself is meditative: She even sings the same song over and over in her head as she creates to stay in the zone. The rituals of creating art help her release feelings because as a self-described "feeler," she becomes easily overwhelmed.

A breast cancer survivor who underwent surgeries and chemotherapy, she used this space as a respite and a chance to become anew. In the months that followed her treatment, the studio was a necessary outlet where she could decompress and work toward her goal of having a solo show just a few months after becoming cancer-free. Having this space helped her create a new art technique while healing: She began sewing ceramic pieces into the art canvas, all because she had a new lease on life and room to invent.

The artist placed her desk near the window to soak in the natural light and boost the happy chemicals in her brain. Art supplies are kept on shelves for easy access and as a source of inspiration. She says that looking at the supplies makes her want to get her hands busy!

DESIGN TIPS

1. When creating a corner where you can recharge, consider serene Scandinavian design. Use chairs with pointed legs and simple oak wood tables as a foundation.

2. Paint your walls white and leave your floors bare. A simple, neutral flat weave rug is the most you'll need underfoot.

3. Pops of blush and black-and-white stripes are common in "modern Scandi" design. Don't be afraid to use color sparingly with this aesthetic.

A task lamp lends an unexpected architectural detail, which feels beautifully organic. The lamp and the minimalist Scandinavian-inspired table and chair work well here, since they don't physically or visually crowd the tiny studio space. And the clean and raw—yet aesthetically thoughtful—nature of the space leaves room for the artist to create.

ABOVE: This ballerina room sashayed from little girl to young woman by way of purple-gray-toned board and batten walls complete with a full wall of mirrors and a ballet bar.

LEFT: Adding a spindle brass bed exudes old world charm. Combine it with floral bedding and a chunky knit throw balances out the softness needed for a metal bed. Adding whimsical pieces like the wooden owl nightstand adds subtle touches of youth without it being too childish.

OPPOSITE: White window treatments with blackout lining help keep the room dark for the restorative sleep kids need. A brass rod adds visual elegance. A chair is always helpful to promote a place of pause. The young lady who lives here starts her day with ballet stretching exercises and breathes in fresh air from the open window nearby as a morning ritual.

manifest your core desire

Goal-making is great, but creating lasting change starts with your thought life and channeling your authentic identity. You already have one tool in your toolbox (see page 30), and you'll soon learn about more tools to help you more easily keep your eyes on the prize. More than anything, you need proof that real change is possible. To me, motivation and good habits are the dynamic duo of accomplishment.

First, the motivation. I've heard this called lots of things like your "why," your "North Star," or your "purpose." For me, I just think of it as connecting to your Core Desire (see page 16). Motivation is sitting at the core of your goal once you peel back the layers and discover what you really crave. You might think you want to lose weight to look hot for your high school reunion, but what you really want is the inner peace that comes with true confidence. You might think you want money, but what you really want is freedom. That Core Desire is what you ride to your destiny. The purpose of the Home Therapy method is to help you discover your Core Desire so that you can sustain your motivation at home in a way that makes you happy and productive.

Multi-tier rolling shelves provide mobile storage for items that you don't always want on display.

Your Core Desire is the big, driving life force that propels you forward to the more fully realized life waiting for you. Cue the triumphant music! But wait. Here's the catch: It's not always easy to connect with an intangible desire like freedom when most of the time you're just lacing up your shoes and hurling your body forward with the grace of a confused baby llama. It's a big, bold, beautiful idea that you need in order to enjoy your best life, but you might need some instant gratification, too. We humans are like that.

Enter small wins.

INTRINSIC   **EXTRINSIC**

Love
Passion
Curiosity
Belonging
Independence

Money
Rewards
Fear of failure
Perfectionism
Others' approval

Healthy relationships
Success
Self-confidence

🧰 Creating Habit Boards

Motivation and small wins are the one-two punch that knocks down your obstacles and helps you reach Goal City. It would be hard to alter our limiting beliefs without at least some "evidence" that our new stories are true, too. Whether it's a motivational quote and Intention Tray, or a stellar workout setup in a corner, we can use our homes to trigger responses, flip our scripts, change behavior, stay motivated, and finally win the lottery! Okay, maybe not the last one, but you can feel like a winner at home.

I once went over to my friend Sarah's house and caught a glimpse of her calendar. Every day had the same simple instructions: No pizza. I asked her about it. Monday's goal: no pizza. Tuesday? You guessed it. No pizza. You get the picture.

HABIT BOARD DESIGN TIPS

1. Turn your wall into a Habit Board with magnetic paint—yes, that's a thing! I love Rustoleum's magnetic paint primer.

2. Paint a thin layer of your favorite paint to cover the magnetic primer (just don't use too much or the magnetism won't work!).

3. Find inspiring pics that represent your goals and post them up with cute magnets.

Now, Sarah is a marathon runner, an award-winning surgeon, and makes all her own baked goods from scratch, which is to say she's no slouch. So why, I asked, did she have such a specific and random goal? She explained that pizza was her nutritional kryptonite, and she felt it would be easier to run the New York City marathon if she was able to shed a few pounds. If she started out with the goal of running a marathon, there was no way to keep the faith that she could actually do that. Eating no pizza for two months straight? Now that was something she could accomplish, and, from there, she'd move on to other, bigger accomplishments with confidence. It's the One Bite Method. *How do you eat a whale?* Answer: one bite at a time.

Now that could mean ten minutes of exercise, one sentence of a novel, or going on two dates a month. The key is consistency and putting your rote brain on

a positive loop. Since I'm in the business of decorating, I created a colorful Habit Board in my visually inviting yoga corner shown in the photos above. Each day I practice here, I get an *X* on the board, and when I reach thirty *X* marks, I treat myself to something special that's within my monthly budget.

Getting yourself on a positive loop with your intentions by cultivating your perfect, personalized space is the key to realizing your Individual Domain. Use the Home Therapy method tools like flipping the script, Intention Trays, journaling, pausing, self-soothing, and Habit Boards to create spaces that serve your individual needs. By growing your confidence through your Individual Domain, you'll be better prepared to get organized and share your space in harmony with others.

HOME THERAPY HOUSE
the individual domain

As we go through this book, I'll be highlighting my ultimate Home Therapy house client project to date. Their Core Desire was to be closer to one another and get to know themselves better. The family room's furniture plan specifically targeted increasing face time away from the TV. The primary bedroom has a custom "me time" zone away from the kids.

ABOVE AND LEFT: A drink table is essential for providing the surface to place a cup of matcha as new discoveries through journaling and reading can be made. Placing a chair in a tight corner works! Trust me. Even though it may seem counterintuitive, having an appropriately sized chair catty-corner from the sofa can invite a new seating area for an individual.

ABOVE AND RIGHT: Finally after years of these homeowners putting themselves last, we cleaned up all the toys, clutter, and laundry out of this room. The partners now have individual areas in the room to find a place to ground themselves. The reading corner has a soft fabric accent chair with ample natural light to boost their serotonin levels in the morning with a fresh cup of coffee. By their bedside, the wood-toned nightstand has plenty of room to hold a tray with essentials, such as their watch and jewelry, as well as an air diffuser that clears the air for restorative sleep and meditation.

PART 2

the organizational domain

Now that you've laid a strong foundation for a therapeutic home with the Individual Domain, it's time to put up those literal *and* metaphorical walls and start creating some structure.

The Organizational Domain will help you further your goal of staying in the present and feeling empowered when it comes to living with your things. Let's be honest—it's really hard to grow, reflect, or feel confident when you're always looking for your other sock or sorting through mismatched Tupperware. In part 2, we're going to break down any mental blocks you have about getting organized. We'll revisit the tidying methods you're currently using, reach a new understanding about why you might default to those methods, and start customizing an organizational system that serves your family's needs. Ultimately, you'll be able to create a home that gives you the structure and security you crave and a sense of calm that will help keep anxiety and depression at bay.

When there are specific parameters in your home that *you* set up, you'll start to feel in control—and maybe even on top of the world! Good organization also means you don't constantly need to create new systems and problem-solve. Your routines are clear-cut and preset, and tidying up becomes rote and easy. That kind of security gives you confidence and bolsters you as you get ready to go out, whether on a date or to a big meeting!

OPPOSITE: Using transparent pendants keeps the eye moving through the space and doesn't interfere with the other design elements. This rope pendant complements the range hood and cane kitchen barstools perfectly.

PREVIOUS PAGE: Linen bedding is breathable and versatile. It's easy to layer, and its natural, textured characteristics make it a very forgiving material.

know your organizing personality

Fun fact! Everyone has a penchant for organizing—not just type A people. And, in fact, the act of organizing isn't about deciding whether to throw out or keep the things you own, as many of us have come to believe. We're not as burdened under the weight of our mothballed sweaters from five seasons ago as we are by the fear and stress brought on by a chaotic world that lets us control some things and not others. It is often our "control misfires" that lead us to a disordered relationship with our things.

We might think an organizational system of boxes and bins will be the answer. It's true that labeling and categorizing might give you a sense of control for a little while, but making peace with what it is you're holding on to is how you'll empower yourself in the long run. Essentially, organizing should not be about making quick decisions about what to do with the "stuff." Instead, it's better to focus on confronting your *relationship* with things you own. It doesn't matter whether you're a minimalist or a maximalist. In the end, your goal is to live in peace, harmony, and balance with everything you own, and that looks different for everyone.

To start, let's look at some of the organizing personalities.

Maximize your storage opportunities in as many spaces as you can. Under-bench space is a subtle solution to storing items you don't use daily.

Savers

I'm often asked what makes a person a saver and what makes someone a tosser, and, suffice to say, it's a bit more nuanced than that. Those who like to hold on to things (we might affectionately call them pack rats) have a tendency toward indecisiveness. Ambivalence is a main reason we find it difficult to let go of things, even if those things negatively impact how we live and function at home. Holding on to things might make us feel like we're in control, but really, we're losing control.

Here are a few reasons you might be a saver:

• You're stuck in the past: You might feel overcome with deep sentimentality for a wide variety of items.

• You're fearful of what's to come: Maybe you are gripped by a belief that saving items will shore you up against unforeseen events in the future, or maybe you're holding on to them so you won't have to rebuy them.

• You feel too guilty to let go: Perhaps you feel bad giving away something that was gifted to you or that something is too expensive to toss.

All of that said, this doesn't need to happen. The Home Therapy method offers therapy-based tools to confront these feelings head-on and move forward in happy, healthy ways.

Tossers

Tossers also feel anxiety and ambivalence about their things. Just like savers, they can experience feelings of helplessness and being overwhelmed, and they might think it's faster to just get rid of something than to think it through. Here's more info about tossers:

• Getting rid of something gives you an instant release and relief from the rising cortisol levels and stress brought on by what you perceive as a mess that needs clearing.

• While tossers tend to be more celebrated than hoarders (your habits are often mistaken for minimalism), you may never have learned how to truly organize your home.

• At a loss for where to put things, you can fall back on your habit grooves and become frustrated when having to rebuy items you tossed a few months earlier.

• You might end up feeling irresponsible and guilty for mindlessly decluttering, but you don't know how to process those feelings in order to break the cycle.

P.S. I'm definitely a tosser! And my husband, Travis, aka Mr. Meticulous, is a saver. So we have to negotiate what is saved and tossed in our home—even if it means Travis going through the toss-away bags that I'm ready to donate to specific organizations or give to other people. He just can't help himself.

Facing Your "Now"

Most of today's popular organizing methods are based on creating "save," "throw," and "donate" piles as we go through our things. While it may be tempting to chuck things from your past that no longer serve you (sayonara ex-whoever!) and bring only bright shiny things into the new future you will create, this strategy assumes we're mostly savers who need to become sorters or tossers, quickly. Because the emphasis is on the past and future, and not the present, the

act of organizing can be only a Band-Aid. There is no moment for contemplation. There is no silence or pause—however uncomfortable that may be—only rapid-fire decision-making. Rarely is the focus on the decision-making itself.

Well friends, from a therapeutic standpoint, there are more helpful and lasting ways to organize your home, but living in the moment, with no guaranteed answers and plenty of uncertainty, can be scary. However, if you start flexing that

ABOVE LEFT: Do your favorite books not exactly match your room's current aesthetic? Store them in a sideboard rather than on the shelf so they stay easily accessible for reading.

ABOVE RIGHT: A bedside cabinet serves as a dressing closet and keeps the clutter out of sight.

muscle when it comes to the things you own, it feels incredible not to have that old movie of the past playing in your head or any fear of the future creeping in.

In order to face the present, you need to clear the space you intend to organize and create a blank slate. If you don't examine *why* you accumulate or purge things, then you will continue the cycle no matter how many times you sort, toss, categorize, or label. Our human tendencies will overtake us, and we'll end up back in the same place. So let's confront our "now" and use a few tools to solve what might be under the hood.

THE HOLDING BOX

Enter the Holding Box, a temporary container to hold your clutter, until you can make decisions about what to do with it. I like to use a pretty woven basket, but the box itself can be any receptacle that works with your décor, whether a beautiful leather case or a clear bin. What's important is that it feels special. This box will hold all your belongings that you're clearing out for twenty-four hours (if you're a saver) or forty-eight hours (if you're a tosser). In the process, it will help you live in the gray, rather than default to black-or-white thinking (keep or toss), so you can practice balancing your attitudes toward your stuff and staying present.

Now pick a small area or surface—like a corner of your family room or a desktop— and clear it out, placing all of the items in the Holding Box. Take in your new blank space. How do you feel about it? Is it uncomfortable to see your space without any of your belongings? Or do you feel

refreshed with the clutter gone? However you feel—good or bad—make peace with those feelings. You want to assess the energy each item brings to the space and whether or not it helps fulfill your goals for this area.

In therapy, we're always talking about assessing your own decision-making. Your goal here is to strengthen your decision-making muscle so you can create a truly intentional and honest home. In essence, consider whether this item meets your needs and goals for one of the domains explained in this book: Individual, Organizational, Communal, or Renewal.

You might ask yourself:

- Does this item empower me as an individual? (Individual)

- Does it help keep my home neater and more organized? (Organizational)

- Does it bring me closer to another family member? (Communal)

- Does it give me a sense of calm or refreshment? (Renewal)

For savers, pay attention to the types of things that you tend to overbuy and hold on to. Are these things serving you? What feeling are you trying to buy? For tossers, what feelings get thrown out, and what gets accomplished (or doesn't) when you do so?

Be honest! Over the next few days, keep thinking about what you want to do with the items. This waiting period—the *not knowing* what you'll end up doing with all this stuff—will likely be uncomfortable, but don't worry. There is a deadline. At the end of that time period, you'll need to take action. After twenty-four to forty-eight hours, you will revisit the items you feel

ambivalent about and decide if you will save or toss them. For the items you save, they have to serve a Core Desire for you or a family member in the home. They should be things that uplift you and have working intentions, not just memories or sentiments. For things that you will toss, identify a person or organization you'll donate them to, or a specific purpose you have for them (old towels for washing the car). Avoid mindlessly throwing items into a black garbage bag for a garbage pickup.

I had a client who had an expensive red dress she was ambivalent about. After a couple of days of keeping it in the Holding Box, she decided to wear it for date nights with her partner, which supported her Core Desire to improve her marriage. Not

only did she think she would never wear that dress again, but she also had long wanted to bring back date night. With some creative thinking and intention setting, she doubled up on her organization and improved her relationship. Talk about a win-win! The smile on her face when I saw her several months later was priceless. The motivation of keeping that dress in her closet was intrinsically positive: There was no way she was going to miss a date with her partner. The tools work!

The Holding Box might seem like a simplistic exercise, but it's a powerful tool. Some of the boxes you'll see in part 2 belong to families confronting intense feelings, as grandparents who lived through the terror of Japanese internment

camps might do, where any possessions were rare or nonexistent. As a result, the homeowners now have trouble letting go of their grandchildren's toys, even in a cluttered space. Others belong to moms who felt attached to baby clothes for varieties of reasons, from difficult births to deciding not to have more children. These are uncomfortable feelings to explore in a twenty-four-hour period, but it's the best

way you can create a genuinely thoughtful home, organize it in a way that will shift the energy, and make it a therapeutic place of clarity. In the end, your space won't be just sorted or coded; it will also tell your authentic story and allow you to grow.

A holding box can be stylish, so you can keep it out in the open and add to it. Here, woven baskets fit in with each room's décor.

Do a Supermarket Sweep

The homeowners of this kitchen live almost an hour from the nearest grocery store, so they really need to stock up. If that resonates with you (or you're super busy and want to shop for food only once in a while) then you know what it's like to organize enough food to fill half of a supermarket. I tidied this client's drawers by recipe categories as opposed to similar items like you find in a grocery store. I also grouped her cannisters by size for more visibility. We often think pantries are for dry goods only, but mixing bowls and measuring spoons can go in here, too, so when you want to make a meal, it's easy to grab everything at once. While grouping like items is useful and attractive, the cornerstone of the Home Therapy method is about creating new loops—and turning healthy meal assembly into an enticing option in the kitchen is one way to break those old patterns. Grouping ingredients together will elicit thoughts of meal creation rather than snacking.

ABOVE: Utilizing pantry doors as additional storage helps keep the excess items off of your countertops.

OPPOSITE: Transparent food containers make it easy to see what's inside so you can quickly grab what you need while cooking.

organize with intention

Earlier in the book (page 17), you noted your Core Desires for a specific space. Now it's time to apply some meaning behind your organization—don't just stuff things away! Whether you add drawer organizers, utilize wall space, or display your collectibles on a shelf, you have plenty of ways to tidy up thoughtfully. Take a look at how these homeowners made the best of their space by intentionally organizing what they needed to help them function and thrive as individuals and as a family.

Instead of thinking that you need to hide your range hood, think about how you can make it pop! Add a unique architectural detail to transform your hood into a beautiful kitchen focal point.

FINDING *MY* CORE DESIRE IN THE KITCHEN

Raise your hand if you recently renovated your kitchen and freaked out the entire time. (My hand is shooting way up in the air right now!) I spent twelve years making small updates to our kitchen—like faux marble countertops—because I had to do *something*. But finally, a decade in the making (movie trailer voice-over), I WAS READY TO RENO. No pressure, right? I made a beeline for Pinterest and started pinning like a fiend. I began vision boarding by figuring out which metals would live in my space (I knew they would be a mix of stainless steel and brass) and then started deciding on the tones that would make sense. I needed to make a budget, consult contractors, and choose cabinet colors and backsplashes.

At first, I pulled pipe-dream kitchen photos (reality check: my kitchen does *not* have a window overlooking the Aspen mountains), but then I began to narrow down the images to photos of kitchens with similar layouts to mine. While I wanted to change the layout of my kitchen, I realized that I didn't need to change the footprint, and it was easier to visualize my reno if I looked at similar spaces. It was also important to me to stay true to my family's needs.

Which leads me to my Core Desire. I knew that before the hammer first hit the wall, I had to figure out my Core Desire in the kitchen. After much soul-searching, it dawned on me that what I really wanted was simplicity and easy flow. I also needed my family to have more agency in the kitchen. I wished to see and reach things and for everything to feel lighter. I really wasn't sure about open shelving at first,

and I was super nervous about keeping it all neat, losing cabinet space, and dishes getting dusty, but I wanted to commit to less clutter and more transparency. The results? Open shelving accomplished everything I needed. It was easy for family and friends to pluck dishes from the shelf, and I trimmed any excess dishes. In the end, it was a game changer.

When determining the flow of my kitchen, I first needed to design it in a close "triangle" setup (made up of sink, refrigerator, and range) so I could move around easily. I then took away my narrow island and added a peninsula because the island blocked the flow. I decided to create stations in order of how I cooked so that I could move through the space seamlessly during meal prep. These would include, in order, from one end of the kitchen to the other:

- dry goods pantry (pasta and spices)
- refrigerator (fresh food)
- appliances (like my food processor)
- pull-out drawers (pots and pans, cooking utensils, cutting boards)
- cooking range
- cabinet (serving platters and plates)
- drawer (cutlery)
- cabinet pull-out (dishwasher and garbage)
- microwave and cabinet in the peninsula for Tupperware (for leftovers)

I created a new story all without taking down a single wall. The best part? You don't need to wait twelve years for a kitchen remodel to create this kind of flow. Just find your Core Desire and let the design follow suit.

Before any renovation project, look at the form and function of your space and consider your WHY. (Hint: Figure out your Core Desire on page 16.)

Open shelving instead of upper cabinets makes the space feel airy.

Compartmentalize Life

I'm sure you know the age-old saying: When in doubt, add a functional drawer pull-out. No? Well, one of the cardinal rules of keeping things from floating away from their proper place is to organize items into the smallest and most visible containers. I find a drawer insert—sized to fit the items it holds—is key to an efficient home. And don't think for a minute this is something that requires custom cabinets. All you need to create this setup is to add inserts and canisters to fit your existing shelves and drawers. This shift will allow you to grab, say, utensils in a way that makes healthy cooking an easy choice. Measure twice, shop once! With good planning you can buy the ones that maximize your space and minimize any frustration of having to go back to the store.

ABOVE: This homeowner enjoys baking on the weekends and wanted to make sure that her favorite baking tools had a special spot to live in. Dedicating an entire drawer to house these items makes for easy access and adding in some organizational trays keeps her favorite tools from getting misplaced.

RIGHT: Organize your beauty products by category. This helps make them easier to find and put away!

SPOTLIGHT
Intention Station

This client uses this space as a backup pantry. (Lucky!) So we made it a welcoming hub for meal assembly and snack storage. From the woven baskets filled with extra table linens to the lazy Susan stocked with nuts for the family, this spot is as functional as it is beautiful. The drawers are filled with containers of healthy snacks, and on top there's a recipe book and plenty of space to prep a meal. There's even a utensil caddy so you can grab a fork and dig in!

ABOVE: The textured finish on this custom cabinet pairs perfectly with the marbled countertop, as they both have an organic appearance.

RIGHT: Only keep out the cookbooks you use frequently. If a lot of them pile up, it can feel daunting and discouraging to try new recipes.

Make Your Walls Work

I think of vertical space and bookshelves as a more intimate layer to your room, as well as an opportunity for more storage. Walls are easily personalized—they can hold favorite books, beloved art and photos, or precious heirlooms. These things line the holding environment that is your home and you want them to reinforce your authentic self. You might hang mirrors for self-reflection or cabinets that hold albums, sentimental notes, or art.

 ## THE STORAGE WALL

From an organizational perspective, a blank wall—or a wall that features art but could be even more useful—can be an opportunity to solve organizing challenges, like where to store kids' backpacks so they don't end up on the kitchen table. The key is to ask yourself what you need in a room and find a blank wall nearby that can help. Take time to think, brainstorm, and process. Let your imagination run wild!

Take inventory of your walls and your organizational problem areas. Where might you be able to hang certain items so they don't end up on furniture or the floor? Could you install wall hooks or pegs in the kitchen for pots and pans, or in the entryway for coats and bags? What about towel hooks in the bathroom? Think beyond the file cabinet in your home office and go for a wall-mounted file organizer. In your home gym, store the yoga mat and hand weights on an exercise equipment rack.

Front hall coat hooks can be for accessories, too! Throw some beads on there for a layered, decorative touch.

ABOVE: Make that family heirloom the star. Add some plants and layer modern accessories to create a focal point.

ABOVE: This storage accessory prevents clutter from showing and allows for easy access to necessary piano items.

OPPOSITE: Stairwells can be opportunities for storage, too! Choose a unique storage unit that can also act as wall art.

MODERNIZING THE MURPHY BED

I decided to transform our guest room into a multipurpose room and was on the hunt for a Murphy bed that didn't just look like a box sitting against the wall. When I couldn't find one, I took matters into my own hands and designed what has become my signature wood-slatted Murphy bed.

When I begin any DIY project, I evaluate the time, energy, and money the project will require. I am all about *not* reinventing the wheel. With this project, we bought a hardware kit for the pull-down mechanics. The I-Semble Vertical-Mount Murphy Bed Hardware Kit with Mattress Platforms from Rockler comes with a mattress support frame and most of the hardware, plus detailed instructions for assembly. After all, the only beef I had with a Murphy bed itself was the door aesthetics. Not the actual mechanics.

If you want to build a door like ours, consider that adding so many extra pieces of wood makes the door a lot heavier and therefore a bit harder to open and shut. Travis can open it by himself but others may find it more strenuous.

MATERIALS NEEDED:

sixty-five ¾-inch poplar wood square slats (for a queen-size bed)

wood glue

brad nails

nail gun

spackle

paint

1. Glue the wood slats onto the door, spacing the slats evenly with a level.
2. Nail the slats in place with a nail gun.
3. Spackle over the nail heads.
4. Paint the wood.

Voilà! You have a beautiful mid-century modern door that looks like a focal point in the room in a subtle yet beautiful manner. For video instructions, scan this QR code.

ABOVE: Color block bedspreads add visual interest without taking away from the patterned area rug. Just make sure to keep the color tones similar!

OPPOSITE: The large brass door handles paired with the wooden slats on the door panels give this Murphy bed an elevated appearance that's so good you can't help but stare!

Adding framed art to the inside of a Murphy bed creates that extra "wow" factor when the bed comes down!

SPOTLIGHT
The Sleeping Wall

In order to turn her garage into a functional guest suite, this homeowner needed the walls to work double duty, so we installed flat-front cabinets and personalized them with acrylic inserts to display her pretty forest photography. We then added open shelving on either side to visually break up the wall and to hold decorative objects or guests' personal items. Finally, we popped in beautiful mid-century chairs, a cozy grounding rug, and a woven side table.

RIGHT: Accent shelving doesn't always need to be heavily layered. Sometimes, less is more.

BELOW: Use furniture pieces that are easy to move as additional seating when your Murphy bed is not in use.

OPPOSITE: This multipurpose guest/office space was the perfect opportunity to play with upper cabinets. Hanging prints on the cabinet doors is a wonderful creative solution to displaying this homeowner's favorite photos.

The Power Corner

There's always a corner that tends to go unused. And what a waste! Real estate is precious—so take advantage of every square foot. Whether it is setting a tray in a kitchen corner with a healthy snack and a meditation candle for a quick pick-me-up, or combining a tall reading chair with a skinny console table for a private reading or working nook, corners can be your secret weapon.

CLOCKWISE FROM TOP RIGHT: Opting for drawers instead of lower cabinets provides more storage opportunities and a modern twist on this hallway niche. • Don't underestimate a narrow console table. Layer in a lamp for ambient lighting, a few baskets for extra storage, and some pieces of art, and you've got yourself a statement corner! • These woven baskets are great for concealing the mess that shoes drag in while giving this mudroom space a natural, organic look.

Floating shelves don't have to be wood! These acrylic shelves show off the wallpaper's entire pattern while giving this homeowner ample space to display their favorite décor pieces.

Hanging Your Things

If you were to ask me the top Home Therapy tool, I would hands down say hooks. They are a genius way to maximize vertical space, even underneath countertops to hold purses or towels. Or you can install rails on kitchen island bases and use hooks to hang pots and pans. Last but not least, pegs are awesome because of their small size—they can be easily installed virtually anywhere.

Not only are hooks on kitchen islands extra convenient for holding dish towels, they can also offer a touch of whimsy in an otherwise muted kitchen.

ABOVE LEFT: Shiplap can be great for a backsplash. The clean lines and neutral colors make the wood counters the focal point of this kitchen.

ABOVE RIGHT: These counter stools are the star of this workspace. They are neutral enough to accommodate kids of all ages, and the sturdy leather material will age well as the kids get older.

OPPOSITE: Believe it or not, this nook used to be a wet-bar. The family had a greater need for a mudroom and a homework station, so here is that vision brought to life. The use of vertical space helps keep the desk space clutter-free.

OPPOSITE: Using different-colored storage bins helps kids understand how to organize toys in different categories, making for quicker cleanup when playtime is over.

LEFT: This white oak shelving looks expensive, but it's actually not! I found these wood shelves at our local lumber store and stained them myself. Pairing the shelving with a brass pendant from Rejuvenation and herringbone pattern tile completes this dreamy kitchen trifecta.

ABOVE: Here's another proud DIY moment. My client didn't know what to do with this awkward vertical space, which just sat empty, collecting dust. I had a wholesale acrylic store cut sheets of acrylic to match the width of the niche for shelving. I chose a statement wallpaper to hang, and all of a sudden an unusable niche transformed into functional homework storage space for this new workstation.

Shelf Awareness

Bookshelves are a practical and flexible way to maximize functionality in a room, nook, or corner. Whether they're built in and recessed with a pretty arch or bought from your favorite home décor store, they are an ideal place to express yourself and your home vibe. The best shelves display at least a few deeply personal objects and tell a story.

To style a bookshelf consider these tips:

1. Add depth. Start by placing larger art in the back of the shelf and then adding medium-sized and then smaller decorative objects toward the front to create multiple layers.

2. Don't forget the books! You can play around with bookends, color-code the spines, or turn the books spine-in for a muted look. Just don't forget to mix vertical with horizontal books to add variety.

3. Anchor the shelves. Place the heaviest (or the heaviest looking) object on the bottom so the shelves won't topple over (or look like they will).

4. Remember that negative space is your friend! We often feel tempted to fill up the whole shelf, but everything needs breathing room. Depending on how long the shelf is, group like objects by twos and threes, and make sure they're differently shaped (think large and small photos or large and small vases). Then add varying amounts of space between groupings.

5. Include a trailing plant or two. Plants like ivy and monstera deliciosa are my go-to for added organic drama. Small potted plants are great fillers as well.

6. Vary your design. Introduce mixed metals for shine or natural elements for texture.

7. Incorporate vintage items or quirky collectibles to let your creativity and personality shine. But use them sparingly: You don't want to run the risk of getting kitschy.

Free-standing bookshelves are your best friend if you change up your spaces often. They're easier to move around and can serve multiple purposes.

CLOCKWISE FROM TOP: Placing armchairs at an angle creates a more intentional conversation space. • Black lower cabinets anchor these built-ins, making them a focal point in this otherwise light and neutral space. • Open shelving can be home to more than just books. Layer in a variety of decorative items to make the space unique to you.

SPOTLIGHT
Boho Bookshelves

In this boho writer's den, we were short on space and wanted to get creative with how we displayed books—both well-thumbed favorites and those she had written or produced herself—so we flanked either side of the mid-century vintage desk with invisible vertical bookshelves. The setup not only proved to be a functional, space-saving choice but also a decorative win.

ABOVE: Hanging artwork should be personal to you, since these pieces are often the first thing people notice when they walk into your home. Take the time to source pieces that hold significance.

LEFT: Wall art doesn't have to be two-dimensional. Getting creative with what takes up the vertical space can help create a focal point.

Floor-to-Ceiling Vintage

It would have been easy to overlook this narrow wall, but the thrift store–loving homeowner utilized this space to the max with a vintage cabinet that quickly became a convenient drop zone. And adding decorative items like a vintage phone and art to personalize the area transformed it from being vertically challenged to hardworking with just a bit of creativity and a dab of ingenuity.

Remember your color wheel! Red-toned woods, blue walls, and gold hardware work together because they are variations of the primary color family.

Say Goodnight

Nightstand organization is your gateway to restorative sleep. The key is to keep this area intentional. Remotes should go in a drawer and phones in a separate charging station. If your phone needs to recharge, then so do you.

This nightstand has an entire calming universe around it with wallpaper that reminds the homeowner of the ocean, and a decorative ladder for extra cozy blankets on cold nights. The open nightstand allows the wallpaper to shine through and also lends breathing room to a small area.

Having a light switch that controls bedside sconces near your headboard provides easy and convenient light management.

Calm the Clutter

These cabinets might look custom, but they're prefabricated, which makes them much more affordable. They work for those who prefer a neater look, and they make sense here in the more formal dining room space. I prefer sturdy cabinetry in an area like this as opposed to a dining hutch or buffet because you can maximize the space from end to end. In this room, we opened up this formerly blank wall with light, bright cabinetry and brass hardware. It's an ideal place for this family to display their tea set and store their artisanal ceramics. This household also had an extra set of "in-between" dishes (neither fancy China nor daily dishware) and the homeowners didn't know where to put them. Now they can use this dinnerware with ease!

Matching your art and accessory colors creates a clean and cohesive visual.

practice makes perfect(ish)

Even though we have established good structure in our homes with hooks, pegs, shelves, and cabinets, it doesn't mean we are done. Our brains rely on us to perform repetitive mind and body functions over and over until they become so natural that we don't even realize we do them anymore. That is truly when something becomes a habit.

With therapy, follow-up is just as important as the actual treatment—you want to set yourself up for success in the long term by maintaining what you've learned. So too with staying organized: You need a maintenance plan for keeping everything in its place. Let's take a look at my Meal Prep Kits and Ski Slope Method before diving into room-by-room examples of organized spaces.

This homeowner had items he wanted to store in his closet, but not necessarily have on display since he didn't need to access them daily. These neutral boxes were the perfect solution since the wooden handles paired perfectly with the drawer trim.

⚒ THE MEAL PREP KIT

I believe the key to all success is pre-planning, and the kitchen is a great place to practice this. As the home therapist, I've seen a lot of messy kitchens. When I notice these spaces in disarray, I know the family isn't eating well, and good nutrition is the foundation for brain health. So before we even get to the feelings stuff, I address this space! Over the years, I've helped my clients with healthy meal planning via meal prep kit trays. First, simply keeping the ingredients together on a tray or in clear bin helps define the task. Second, having the utensils and measuring spoons and cups on the tray makes them more accessible and saves you time. Third, having all the cookbooks placed near the trays and online recipe bookmarks on an iPad or printed and kept nearby takes the guesswork out of what's for dinner. (If you're lucky enough to have a smart fridge that has a screen, it is such a lifesaver! We had one, and the girls loved saving recipes, writing notes, and accessing Pinterest and online recipes quickly.) It's easier to wrap your mind around cooking dinner if all of the components are conveniently contained—so staying on your positive loop becomes more intuitive.

It's also simpler to tackle the concept of one meal, as opposed to a whole pantry of food—especially when you have to throw a meal together at the last minute! Don't depend on your tired self to make the right decisions. Pick a morning or night when you can create these for the week. Even if you already use meal delivery kits, it's still important to add meal prep kits to your daily habit list so you can personalize, customize, and take ownership over meal time. You can post the menu somewhere in your kitchen to prepare your family as well.

DESIGN TIP

I don't subscribe to a one-size-fits-all spice rack for kitchen organization. For multicultural families (like mine), I like to separate out my Asian spices, Italian spices, and then my staples for easier meal prep. Spices are major tools for making healthy food taste good, so make sure you have an easy-grab pantry station, wall rack, lazy Susan, or drawer pull-out for organizing spices.

CLOCKWISE FROM TOP LEFT: Waterfall countertops are a subtle way to keep texture moving in your kitchen space. • Organization trays in your pantry make meal prepping even quicker. • Wood serving dishes make food look even more appetizing and enhance the organic features of fruits and vegetables. • Color is just as important when it comes to your food! Having a variety of fresh, bright options makes eating healthy all the more exciting.

OPPOSITE: Options are endless when it comes to custom cabinetry. You don't need to keep everything on the countertop—think of creative ways to store your kitchen essentials.

THE SKI SLOPE METHOD

As a therapist, when I would go see clients, I could tell when clutter or disorganized emptiness was contributing to the problems they were working through. Their things made them feel blocked and trapped, and I needed to come up with an organizing method that didn't overwhelm them. After all, these clients were under enormous pressure in their lives, and I needed to make living well easier for them, not harder.

At the same time, I was a new mom, and my kids' rooms would fill with toys and clutter. It would drive me crazy, but with all the other things I had to do, tidying up was hard to maintain. The fifteen-minutes-a-day cleanup trick felt like a game of whack-a-mole where nothing ever truly felt finished! The massive, overwhelming cleanse wasn't going to work either because of my tight schedule. With growing girls, I simply couldn't organize or purge to a place where I never had to tidy. Out of necessity, I slowly began to adopt a new mindset and strategy for straightening up. I now call this the Ski Slope Method.

Cleaning is a mental marathon, and if not for this cognitive trick, I probably would have either thrown everything away or given in to the clutter, but this new method worked! I began to teach this technique to my interior design clients and my therapy clients alike.

The idea is to imagine your messy room like a ski slope. If you try to go straight down, the steep angle feels scary and overwhelming. But if you traverse the slope—skiing from one side to the other—you lessen the angle and make it down the

mountain without even noticing. Instead of looking at the room from front to back, look at it from corner to corner.

Start in one corner of the room and tidy it up. When that section is clean, move to the other side of the room, like you would traverse a mountain. Clean that area and move back to the other side as you work your way "down" the room. Once I began teaching this method, I realized that each time I visited my clients, their homes were neater or more organized. And once my clients realized they could tackle rooms in chunks and still get the whole room done, they were able to achieve clean rooms, too. Not knowing where to begin is where many people give up. Using this method, your brain believes you're going to make it down the slope, so you keep going!

OPPOSITE: Layering an area rug, artwork, and accessories can make an entry bench the star of the show.

organize in every room

I'm hoping the Home Therapy organizational tips on the following pages give you an added layer of security and structure to apply to all the rooms in your home. As a designer and therapist, I have found that structure is the key to a solid foundation and it simply can't happen on its own. You must take steps to build that structure if you want to feel secure and happy from the inside out. Rome wasn't built in a day, so just start by showing up every day. Take one step at a time in cleaning up your messy drawer or kitchen counter. Then one day you'll notice you're actually doing it: You are organized. You've got this!

When styling your shelves, consider the scale of your items. Placing larger-scaled items at the bottom, midsize items on the middle shelf, and smaller items on the top shelf creates balance and movement throughout your shelves.

Entryways

The entryway is the perfect place to check in with yourself, pause, and connect with the identity you want to embody. It is a transient space, but one that has to work hard to help you transition from the outside world to your home. So ask yourself what kind of person you want to be when you leave your home. Who do you want to be when you come back to your family? Contemplate this while you put on your shoes or hang up your coat. On your way out the door in the morning, the entryway should empower and energize you, and in the evening, it should relax and soothe you upon your return. You should have space here to store keys, mail, and grab-and-go items like umbrellas and dog leashes. It also helps to have an inspirational quote to ground you even if it's just in a bowl on a bench. Having all of this on hand will make the act of coming and going easier so you can focus on your mindset and practice being present.

Here are some questions to ask yourself while you're in the entryway:

- How do you feel when you leave the house?

- How do you feel when you come back home?

- Is there a pattern here that you're not happy with?

- How can this space help you break that pattern so you can stay present at home?

OPPOSITE, ABOVE: Sometimes less really is more. The modern artwork, chandelier, and railings truly all speak for themselves.

OPPOSITE, BELOW: This homeowner wanted to create a statement in the entryway, rather than have it be cluttered with shoes and jackets. We moved the functional grab-your-stuff-and-go space to a different entrance and curated this vision of an entry! She loves how open and inviting this area is for guests to walk into.

LEFT: Layering soft textures on a hard piece of furniture makes it feel more inviting.

RIGHT: The spindles on the bench mimic the stairway balusters, creating a beautiful motif throughout this small space.

SPOTLIGHT
Clear & Minimal

The homeowner in this space wanted a super minimal entryway but her kids kept dropping their skateboards, backpacks, and shoes on the floor because there was nowhere else to put them. Sound familiar? The client thought hooks would look messy and unattractive, but she was ignoring, rather than confronting, the problem that the space was getting messy *because* there was no organizational system. We had to address her mindset just as much as we needed to fix the space.

The client and I first discussed the black-and-white thinking that led to her belief that the space could either be beautiful or functional. She agreed to open her mind. The simple rack of hooks we added was a game changer, and the extra-large basket to the side of the entryway created a place for shoes and skateboards. We also added a bowl for mail, keys, and an inspiring quote. We finished the space with a short ladder to hold dog leashes, and a plant to make coming home a calmer and more welcoming experience. The homeowner saw how attractive the space looked and how easy it was to keep tidy! She changed her story and saw what was possible.

Get creative with your entryway! Try a leaning mirror with some floor accessories instead of the go-to console table.

The bright red in the area rug makes this bold cabinetry feel intentional by keeping the strongest color moving throughout the space.

Cheery in a Flash

The family in this home wanted an invigorating entryway to bring energy to their space. It features lockers for each member of this high-octane blended family of seven. With so many busy family members coming in and out like a revolving door, the different-sized clothing and shoes in need of organized storage was constantly piling up on the floor. It is no wonder the family customized large lockers like this one right off the entry way. Now there's a place to hang jackets as well as an area for storing hats and shoes. But the extra-special thing about these lockers is the opening in the bottom, which leads straight to the laundry room. Each family member can put dirty clothes directly down the shoot and into a personal hamper that sits in the laundry room below. Not only does everyone take responsibility for their own clothing, but it's also easy and fun to transport dirty clothes to the washer. While this might seem luxurious, anyone with a laundry room directly below their entryway can construct a chute! Or simply add a pretty and discreet laundry hamper in the entryway for kids to drop their muddy tees or socks.

The Kitchen

Often called the heart of the home, the kitchen is also an incredible opportunity for personal growth. It's just one big playground and lab for learning how to organize yourself physically, structurally, and emotionally. Everything from containers to labels to baskets can be organized, but your internal domain needs to align as well. These days, the kitchen is a place to make meals, preside over homework, hold court and entertain friends, or just sit and work or read. For some people (okay: me), this space can be a mixed bag. While I love the warm comfort that is the beating heart of the home, I also really love the warm comfort of glazed doughnuts. For me, the kitchen holds a duality—it is both functional and relational.

If I'm feeling frustrated and behind the eight ball and I find myself in the kitchen, bread and pasta are an escape from the feeling that I'm not on top of everything. I end up eating my overwhelm or boredom in the form of leftover spaghetti. Who's with me? But I've come to know what my triggers are in the kitchen and how to counteract them. What are yours? What is your kitchen not doing for you, and what do you wish it did? For me, I know that if I head to my Individual Domain spot and fix the feelings that trigger me to overindulge, then I don't need the food as much. Let's experiment together in this space and use organizational methods as our tools.

This oven appliance is an absolute dream in this kitchen. It gives space an updated facelift without taking away from the existing charm.

RIGHT: A caffeination station was this homeowner's dream. Before she created this structure, everything was on the countertop and it was always messy. Now these pocket doors slide out and then fold so that after her morning ritual she can close them and this area disappears. She keeps the area tidy, though, so that she always has the option to leave the doors open for when she's entertaining guests.

OPPOSITE: We placed the homeowner's most used cookbooks on open shelving around the vent hood for easy-to-grab inspiration, recipe checks in the middle of cooking, or making grocery lists. The shelves are short, but we opted for them anyway because this kitchen is relatively small and we wanted to allow for some breathing room. Closed cabinets can sometimes be confining and alternating them here gave the right balance.

This Light of Mine

This was a super narrow pantry, so we utilized every inch. We focused on arranging the most-used items so they're easy to reach. Then, on the floor, we turned our attention to bulk items like paper towels and grocery bags. One of the things I love most about this pantry is the natural light pouring in through the window sliver. It would have been simple to grab for extra storage and forego the light, but this couple made an intentional choice to avoid cramming in more things! They prioritized their happiness and the dopamine that sunshine brings.

Another special and functional element in this pantry are the woven rolling baskets. It's so easy to take things out of this space and wheel them elsewhere in the house. Finally, I added a single 3M hook for reusable grocery bags. Allow yourself to think high and low when you're looking for solutions, even in a space you want to be pretty—the hook doesn't steal this pantry's beauty! It simply adds function.

Symmetrical shelving and accessory placement creates a balance that the eye is drawn to.

SPOTLIGHT
Food Hub

Welcome to the Yokota food hub, where I stay focused on empowering my children. My tween loves to make pancakes for our family on Saturdays, so to make this easier and more fun (for her *and* for me), I put everything she needs on the top shelf. For my youngest, I even made a PB&J tray with a kid-friendly knife. I also divide their snacks into baskets for each of them, and they know their parameters. They can have anything in their bins three times a day—a great trick that even works for adults!

Think about the height of your food boxes and storage containers when determining the placement of your pantry shelves.

SPOTLIGHT
Meet the Micro Kitchen

No space is too small for open shelving. It's particularly useful in a tiny guest kitchenette because items are displayed and easily found. When we designed this, we wanted the ceiling to look higher, so I paired the shelving with wall-to-ceiling tile that also acts as a backsplash. In addition, the custom concrete countertops with their etched edging make the otherwise all-white micro kitchen unique.

Offsetting these floating shelves provides movement that plays with the tile behind it, creating a visual that the eye naturally follows.

Choose a strong fixture as the character piece for a smaller kitchenette, like this brass sink faucet.

The Bathroom

The bathroom plays a big role in your positive loop as well as your self-confidence. It's a space central to personal development because it's typically the first room you go into when you wake up and the last place you're in before you slip into bed at night. This is where you look in the mirror, perhaps where you weigh yourself, and where you go as an escape to relax with a bath or long shower. It's also a place for daily maintenance habits, such as skin care and teeth brushing. A thoughtful daily routine in the bathroom can elevate these habits, especially if you organize everything according to your intentions.

I combined current (and potential) rituals with functionality to make this space really sing. Just like in the kitchen, I like creating kits based on the way you live. That could entail taking a humdrum face-washing task and turning it into a full-fledged skin care ritual by incorporating an Intention Tray with your day and night products on either side of it, along with a quote about being comfortable in your own skin. In my bathroom, for example, along with my serum, moisturizer, and mask, I include incense and sage that I use when I perform this ritual so it's all in one spot. You can create foot care kits (mine has a pumice stone, cream, overnight foot mask, and sage) or up your mani/pedi game this way. The goal is to evoke an organized spa-like experience.

On the next level, I like to up the "grab factor" on items that you *could* use more but might forget unless they're in your direct line of vision. For me, that's things like floss and exfoliant. I also leave room for new products and needs by keeping a healthy dose of flexibility in my bathroom organization. That's why I prefer broad labeling categories for drawer organization rather than super specific. If very specific labeling helps you, then more power to you! But my life changes too often to color inside the lines in that way. For instance (to actually use the coloring analogy), I used to separate my daughter's coloring box into pencils, crayons, and markers. Now it's just called "Natalie Coloring." And one day she won't want to color and the bin will be used for something else, but it will be a *whole thing* for me to change it. For that reason, I love moveable drawer dividers over serious labeling.

THIS PAGE: Corral smaller items into a tray so you're less likely to misplace them.

OPPOSITE: This framed shower door adds a lot of character to a small bathroom space. Carrying that black finish through the sink, hand towel, and shower tile details makes a very bold visual statement.

SPOTLIGHT
Go with the Flow

Before we created this Zen retreat, the couple hadn't made any changes to their bathroom in thirty years. *Thirty.* Don't do that, friends. Even if you don't have the funds (who does?), you can always update a vanity, change out a mirror, or add wallpaper. No more black-and-white thinking!

So for the long-awaited overhaul of this bathroom, I aimed to make it beautiful *and* to add in a flow. We designed zones, much the way I designed my kitchen. I began with the his-and-hers sink space, then the bathtub chill zone, followed by the shower zone. I often design bathrooms the Japanese way, imagining the homeowner will want to take an exfoliating bath before a shower. I am adamant about using ladder pull handles for showers because if there's no place to put a towel bar you can hook your towel there. Last, we designed the vanity area. The client's Core Desire here was to feel beautiful on the inside and out and to have a place to feel feminine in a house with three sons, and we organized all the drawers and cabinets to reflect the zone flow and to make this happen.

ABOVE: Adding cane detailing into these cabinet doors creates texture and is a great way to incorporate an organic feel.

OPPOSITE, CLOCKWISE FROM TOP LEFT: Shower niches provide ample storage for your shower necessities and eliminate the need to hang caddies on your beautiful fixtures. • Area rugs provide a soft and delicate contrast to the harsh lines of cabinetry and hardware in a bathroom. • Neutral towels help make sure your bathroom finishes pop! • When making a statement with tile in your shower, make sure to use fully transparent glass doors so you can really appreciate the detail when not in use.

DESIGN TIPS

1.   If you have room, place a stool or rack near your tub to hold a towel and a healing crystal or book.

2.   Drawer pull-outs are not just for the kitchen—they work in the bathroom, too! Consider installing them where the cabinets meet the corners to improve access.

3.   Go horizontal. I prefer horizontal shower niches rather than vertical because they allow for more space, especially when two people are sharing. Before creating a shower alcove, I bring the clients' current shower products to the contractor and ask them to size the alcove to fit the height of the tallest bottle. If you're not undergoing a construction project, consider adding horizontal shelves or corner open shelves before resorting to a shower caddy.

You can place an Intention Tray anywhere—even on your bathtub! Take this time to use some aromatherapy elements and be intentional about what you keep on display.

SPOTLIGHT
Divide and Conquer

I like to use dividers in every drawer, but they don't always have to be clear or white. I went with a little color psychology and chose these tray colors because I thought they were soothing. They make me even happier when I open my drawers. Tonal inserts help compartmentalize and organize my Core Desires for myself, too. This emotional organization is very helpful for me in setting specific intentions for each day, especially if I have an important work goal coming up or a life milestone I want to celebrate or work toward.

LEFT: The black outlets match the black hardware on the drawers. Even small details like this contribute to making the design feel intentional.

ABOVE: Store your go-to bathroom items in the drop drawers for easy access.

OPPOSITE, ABOVE: Using large-scale mirrors in the bathroom is functional, a nice wall statement, and is great for reflecting natural light.

OPPOISTE, BELOW: Opt for a semi-open cabinet in your bathroom to display your visually pleasing accessories and go-to essentials.

To make your guests feel welcome, set out practical products like toothbrushes, canisters for Q-tips and cotton balls, and a bottle for water. Add palo santo, crystals, and a candle. Done.

Keep infrequently used items, such as extra towels, additional hand soap, and cleaning supplies, behind closed cabinet doors.

Bedroom & Closets

For all you maximalists, closed nightstands can signify calm. You're so open with your possessions in the rest of your home that you might want a visual break from looking at "stuff" before bed. Sconces allow for more nightstand surface area (which I promote whenever possible). It's always good to edit your nightstand to just three items—a sculpture for inspiration, a plate or bowl for smaller items, and a reading lamp or other soft light. Form, function, and ambiance.

LEFT: Pitchers can be nightstand décor! Throw some pretty branches in there and it becomes an upcycled vase.

ABOVE: A neatly organized walk-in closet plays double-duty as an inspiring workout nook.

OPPOSITE: Closed drawer nightstands contain all the essentials for a healthy restorative sleep ritual without any clutter. Place only intentional items on the tabletop to help you manifest your Core Desire. Whether it is a modern design with scalloped features or a traditional dresser nightstand for larger beds, long horizontal drawers with unique hardware add something special to your bedroom vibes.

MY CLOSET SAGA

Just looking at photos of this closet still gives me a twinge of anxiety. I play an old movie in my mind in which we move into our house and our oldest daughters are both under two. This movie has a cool sepia filter, and I'm desperately trying to make the closet work for me. Years go by, seasons change, my hair gets longer and shorter, and all the while I'm buying bins and baskets (and even a massive IKEA wardrobe I place in between my girls' twin beds). Six years pass while I am shoving toys and clothes and linens into different configurations until finally I have baby number three and realize I can't go through it again. I decide to invest in an Elfa closet system and my life changes.

No, this is not an Elfa commercial. It's an infrastructure public service announcement.

I wanted so desperately to save the money it would cost to put in a closet with the kinds of shelves and drawers and hanging potential that this closet now has. The thing is, there is no doubt I spent as much or even more on baskets, bins, and stand-alone wardrobes, not to mention time. Sometimes there is no substitute for structure, no hack that rivals creating a sound baseline.

Before you start any project, I implore you to look at the base. It's great to take things out of a drawer, sort through them, and then put them back neater than they were before, but the better exercise is to ask yourself: Is this the right drawer? Is this the right system? Is there a better way? Be mindful. Be intentional, and don't be in denial like me.

Now, with this system, I can clearly communicate to my children what goes where. There is less fighting and more space for their purses, bags, and overnight backpacks. I try to hang everything I can, and when I can't, I put things like underwear and socks and toys in the drawers. Mornings are easier. The room is cleaner, and it was all worth it.

I love a customizable closet system that grows with the kids. Here are some fun tips for kids' closets:

1. I use DIY ceiling track curtains as closet doors because they make it easy for two people to access the closet at once (my girls share)! You can always make it fun with a bright color or pattern.

2. Allow the kids to pick an exciting paint color for the inside of the closet walls. The more invested they are, the more incentive they have to stay organized. You want them to own their space.

3. Use drawers for underwear, pjs, and socks. I try to hang as many tops, sweaters, dresses, and pants as possible to make it easy to sift through. If hanging isn't possible, this is where labeling comes in handy because you can make a note when an article of clothing is "capri legging" versus "full legging" or if a shirt is short sleeved or long and you won't have to pull everything out.

Using curtains in lieu of closet doors is child-friendly and adds a softer touch to this little girl's bedroom.

SPOTLIGHT
Managing Maximalism

The owner of this compact apartment loves stepping out dripping in jewelry and accessories, so he creatively organized his tiny 1930s closet. He uses the closet rod as a necklace holder, clothespins to hold scarves, and pegs for hats. He added a mirror for a full dressing moment, along with inspiring decorative objects like art and plants. This proves that a clean closet doesn't have to be boring. It can be teeming with personality and style and still feel neat and organized.

ABOVE: This dresser top is the perfect place for this homeowner to display his sentimental items that he doesn't necessarily need on display in the rest of his home. He can take some time to appreciate the nostalgia these items bring as he gets ready for the day.

BELOW: Color-blocking the wall paint colors contributes to giving this closet character! The colors complement the dresser, which helps establish balance and cohesion.

OPPOSITE: Dressers provide ample storage in your closet if you don't have a custom organization system. Use a tall dresser to maximize the space.

DESIGN TIP

I like to organize my clothes from light to dark, much like the paint light reflective value going from 0 (black) to 100 (white). Then I arrange by fabric from lightest (think tank tops) to heaviest (sweaters) within the color. So the heaviest white sweater ends the white color section. This might not work for everyone, but I love it. Try it!

This look lets you show off your clothes like you're "going into wardrobe" before your television debut. This is a great solution if you love your clothes but don't have enough space for them, you want to use your closet for something other than clothes (no limiting beliefs about "rooms" here), or you want to celebrate being a minimalist. The lesson here is that organizing looks different for everyone, but it should make you happy, and you should know where everything is.

Closet Reboot

This couple's primary bathroom was stuck in the 1980s and needed a makeover, stat. The closet had been in the middle of the bathroom and blocked the flow. We moved it to a side space, reconfigured the door entry, and opened up the bathroom. Then we added pocket doors and assigned each partner a side of the closet. I brought in these leather baskets for an added organizational and design element. I love adding different textures in any room—even a closet—and the warm walnut tone here picked up on the color of the bathroom vanity. Because we didn't label the baskets, I explained it was important to keep the categories super specific in this case— handbags and ball caps, for example. Lastly, the closet had worn carpet, so I popped in a small 3-by-5-foot kilim rug to complement the leather. Anything that makes your closet fun to walk into will encourage your brain grooves to lean into positive motivation and action. And you know what that means—you might actually stay organized!

ABOVE LEFT: Baskets in a wire drawer help contain smaller items neatly. Underwear, socks and even headbands can be identified efficiently.

ABOVE RIGHT: A robust closet organizational structure makes a world of difference in gaining that dopamine hit of staying tidy. The answer to sustaining neatness in closets is to have the power of flexibility to rearrange the configuration as you grow in your identity.

OPPOSITE: No worries if you can't move your closet shelves, use different baskets as a way to code items and essentials. Leather baskets and woven baskets can serve different purposes for your organizational Core Desire.

The Laundry Room

I get that most of us think of laundry as a chore and to hear someone say they love doing dishes or wiping down countertops can inspire eye rolls. But I have to tell you I truly love doing laundry. Perhaps that's because I made my laundry room (and by laundry room, I mean space in the garage) a haven by including Rebecca Atwood wallpaper, DIY Ikea cane cabinets, and porcelain countertops. But my love of spin cycles is also rooted in my mindset.

I think of laundry as a cleansing ritual and as a time to begin anew. I find that seeing the clothes spin has a meditative effect and I even say little positive affirmations while I wait. Sounding like a housewife in a 1950s commercial yet? Before you turn the page, I at least want you to try it. It's honestly one of the few moments I get some peace and quiet to myself! This won't work for everyone, and if dumping in the jumble of darks and whites and dousing it all with detergent before you run back to a reality show is your style, there's absolutely nothing wrong with that. But if you want to embrace the idea of laundry as a meditation, you might get some "pause" time out of this.

One of the first ways I'm able to accomplish this is that as soon as my kids were able to do their own laundry, I made sure that went on their to-do lists. I even have a tongue-in-cheek sign that reads SELF-SERVICE at our laundry station. That means I'm not constantly running to the machine piling in load after load. So when I do find myself performing this cleansing ritual, it's actually relaxing. Each family member should do their own laundry because it's empowering for them, and it takes the literal and metaphorical load off of you.

I started small by teaching my kids to put their dirty clothes together when they were very young and to bring their hampers to the laundry room. Then I placed detergent and dryer balls in tall baskets on the open shelves so all the tools anyone would need to throw in a load were there. That way everything was all set up; and the more set up you are in this area, the closer you are to my blissed-out laundry mindset.

DESIGN TIPS

1. Keep all your heavily used laundry tools (detergent, stain remover, and wool dryer balls) on a basket tray on top of the laundry machines.

2. Use tall baskets on open shelves to hide your bulk items.

3. Put a day on the calendar to wash, dry, fold, and put away. Washing can be easy, but organizing it back into closets sometimes takes weeks. Yes, I see you!

4. Make the space interactive with notes or quotes on a board.

5. Store linens, winter blankets, or guest towels you're not using.

6. Keep cleaning supplies in labeled baskets so you can pull down the entire basket and grab what you need.

Raise your laundry machines, especially the front-loaders! Better for your back and easier to manage those heavier loads.

LEFT: This hidden laundry station—centrally located but behind doors—hits on so many things I love about functional, inviting laundry spaces. First, the green cabinetry is earthy. (We often think that laundry or kitchen spaces automatically have to be white, but this is a great place to personalize with color.) I also adore the storage, a rod for hanging, and clean and dirty baskets on wheels from Pottery Barn.

OPPOSITE: Don't have a limiting belief about where your laundry machines can go! This family added machines in the bedroom hallway leading to their bathroom. While this could have otherwise just become another closet, they chose to set themselves up for cleaning success with this added convenience. I kept the flooring the same throughout multiple spaces to establish a cohesive flow.

Laundry Without Limits

My laundry space is the builder's afterthought. It is situated in the garage, and my car literally butts up in front of the machines when parked, so I had to make this space as inviting as I could to feel motivated to even bring my dirty clothes out here to wash! I also needed a nice large space to fold the clothes; otherwise, they would be on my bedroom floor in huge piles waiting for my family members to pluck out their daily outfits.

That's why I went with open shelving. I use high baskets to hide detergent, cleaning products, and the iron and steamers. I also brought in kitchen canisters instead of detergent canisters. The wallpaper also makes it feel homey. But my IKEA cabinet doors are my pride and joy. At one point—with the brass fixtures and porcelain countertops that frame the machines and act as a folding station—this was nicer than any other room inside my house! With all this, it's laundry heaven.

WFH Havens

Whether you work from home (WFH) or need a feed-your-mind bonus space, you may want to set aside an area where you can focus and be productive.

We spend so much time at work that it's impossible not to be affected by this space. When you're creating a new work-from-home area, think carefully about how important natural light is. Try to get close to a window or install a skylight if you're able.

For me, good lighting—whether in the form of natural light or recessed and task lighting to brighten the whole room—is necessary in a home office. I'm also a huge proponent of wall organizational systems, wall hanging folders and calendars, and as many boards as possible. A wall clock also brings concrete accountability as the hours pass. And I like to use trays and dishes rather than typical plastic containers for office supplies because they're homier and give you more design opportunity. And don't forget plants!

ABOVE: Anchor desk accessories with a tray to prevent clutter.

OPPOSITE: This multifunctional space started out as a garage and became a home office. The adjustable-height rolling desk and stool allow for this versatility: You can work standing up or sitting down. Want a rolling desk for yourself? All we did was buy the IKEA desk and caster wheels from the local home improvement store. Easy peasy!

Dual Desks

To maximize the full potential of a small space, customize your desk setup. In this tiny WFH nook, I chose mostly closed cabinetry, but I added some open cabinetry to break it up because a wall of doors could end up swallowing the space. I also wanted some room for items that need to be within easy reach, hence the laptop holder, which acts as a shelf when we're not using it for the computer.

For our family, we needed the dual space for both a desktop and laptops, so the L-shaped layout of the desk made the most sense. And because being able to see your work is paramount in a space meant for productivity, I splurged on under-cabinet lighting.

This wall grid helps with my productivity because I can easily post to-do lists as well as vision board items. Then there's the pin board, which serves as my daughter's personal inspo place, and I went all-in here with magnetic dry-erase boards and wall ledges. I even keep a "feeling" vocab chart up here so as I'm sitting in this space, it's easy to check in with myself and pinpoint what I'm feeling so I can uncover what might be stifling me from reaching work goals. I added plants because research shows plants help increase concentration and focus. Lastly, I finished with an office Intention Tray complete with pencils. This compact space packs a big punch!

Mixing open shelves with upper cabinetry creates an opportunity to display more of your favorite decorative objects.

SPOTLIGHT
Screen Time Symmetry

Remember that shared vertical bathroom mirror from page 145? This is the same couple! Pretty amazing, right? This decorating duo intentionally carved space out of the hallway to help them unwind at night and have a screen time stopover before heading to the bedroom where no electronics are allowed after ten o'clock.

Books on the floor create a kind of perimeter that sets boundaries (they don't have to be messy or an afterthought). Here they are an intentional way to organize by using the extra floor space. These homeowners are design fanatics, so all these books are about design. Also, check out the hexagonal light therapy lamp that mimics real sunlight. I would be happy to have this double desk as part of my home office space!

Don't underestimate those window sills! Most sills are just wide enough to accommodate your favorite books or a small potted plant.

This father of five uses après-work enrichment time in his home office to learn how to be a better leader. Here he reads business articles and keeps up on industry news—it's kind of like a feed-his-head-and-answer-his-emails spot.

While his job isn't often a creative one in the artistic sense, his desk holds an inspirational framed picture of Mick Jagger, his favorite rocker. The photo reminds him of fun times and provides him with a Core Desire for all his hard work. He also added a mini air purifier, a tiny lamp (for mood setting and ambient light), a box of special notes from his wife, and a calming candle.

His desk organization is guided by slim-lined cabinets; the wider corner houses a clock. The great thing about extra desk space is that you can get more creative than with your primary work desk. You don't need a photo of your family because they're right down the hall. So instead, opt for an image of your own Jagger. Have some fun.

Keep candles and diffusers near your workspace for aromatherapy moments throughout the day.

DESIGN TIP

Steer clear of decorative objects on top of cabinets like these. They usually just end up collecting dust. Instead, opt for lidded boxes for extra storage that's easy to pull down.

SPOTLIGHT
We Work Here

When I renovated my kitchen, I wanted to add an extra zone on the other side of this peninsula as a secondary place to work. I don't recommend the kitchen as a primary work-from-home station; but this is a good fallback spot. Ideally, I wanted custom filing cabinets, but "ideally" doesn't always work out. Instead, I found these baskets and bins from Target to hold my design supplies, paint swatches, and textiles. All the clutter that previously lived on my kitchen island has now found a home, and I've never looked back.

DESIGN TIPS

1. Make sure to measure your space before you go shopping for organization containers.

2. Check online to see what kind of containers will work with your space. This eliminates A LOT of guesswork, panic, and impulse buying.

3. Create a checklist on paper or on your phone. With that in hand, when you go shopping for your items, you can feel confident in knowing that what you are purchasing is going to work.

ABOVE: If your kitchen counter doubles as your workspace, use the lower cabinets to store your essential home office supplies.

OPPOSITE: Who said your outlets have to stay on the wall? Hide them in your countertop!

When I was a therapist for families with teenagers, I learned that some of the biggest struggles tended to be about devices and device time. So I introduced a rule where we picked a neutral part of the home and the kids had a device curfew, meaning devices needed to be charging in that spot by 9:00 p.m. If they weren't, then they lost their device privileges the next day.

Setting boundaries is great because everyone understands the structure and parameters. I have a lot of parameters surrounding social media and screen time, and I use my organizational tactics to help me in the form of drawers, baskets, and centrally located charging stations. In my home, I didn't want to interrupt my tile, so we created these hidden outlets and USB ports. At first, I was met with lots of protest over these rules, but having tangible things to point to—like charging stations—really helped. Now it's a family habit!

Establishing structure in your home contributes to feeling more organized and will help you take back control. The key to mastering the Organizational Domain is identifying why your current methods aren't working and really being intentional about creating new methods that meet your Core Desire. Remember that your overall goal is to make sure your new tidying tactics, organizational systems, and screen-time house rules are practical and sustainable. Implementing these Home Therapy tools will ultimately create space for quality, communal time to share with your loved ones. (Read part 3 to learn more about that domain!)

the organizational domain

"It takes as much energy to wish as it does to plan," so said Eleanor Roosevelt. In the Home Therapy House, the family transformed their wish for a neat and organized home into spaces that were intentionally and meticulously planned. We had post-it notes all around the kitchen and pantry and in the bathroom before even the cabinets were made or the Elfa closet system hung. With their Intake Form in hand, we gathered intel and created storage opportunities so their serotonin levels would level up.

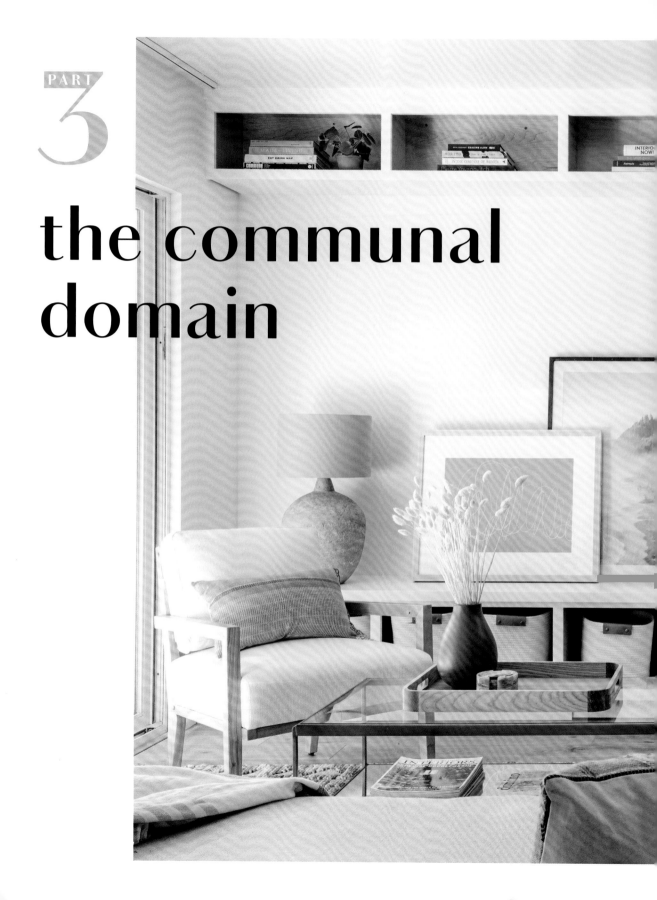

the communal
domain

I was a marriage and family therapist for almost two decades before turning to interior design, so this is kinda my thing. I've seen it all. And as your therapist, I know that elevating your relationships is the next step in our work together.

You've connected with your individual needs and cleared space to be present. You then created structure through organization. Now it's time to reach outward to the other people living in your home because honestly, it's these interpersonal relations that truly make a house a home. So if you can't remember the last time you stared deep into your partner's eyes, or you only get one-word answers out of your teenager, or you just wish you could bring back game night with friends, then this domain will speak to you, big time.

Our most intimate moments and deeply felt personal talks are had at home, which is why this next step in the Home Therapy method— addressing the personalities and interactions happening inside

your (now highly organized and personalized) walls—is so important. We often have a dreamy idea that the foundation of a healthy relationship is automatically set in place, like in a rom-com. Reality is way more methodical and definitely has fewer meet-cutes. IRL, you have to build a relationship one step at a time and build trust over time. In this section, we'll explore using these tools to elevate our relationships to dream levels, as well as to increase social skills and face time. In my practice, I believe there are five main characteristic groupings that make up a stellar relationship. They are: communication and connection, playfulness and trust, boundaries and self-care, mentoring and teamwork, and love and gratitude. In this domain, we'll take a look at how to achieve all of these using your home.

We'll use tools like feelings words and communications scripts to confront tension and hone conflict-resolution skills, situate furniture for maximum connection, set boundaries using décor parameters, elevate game rooms, and more. Whether we're working on making the dining table a hub for positive communication or the living room a place for play therapy, the goal here is to use your

home to strengthen bonds with family and friends. We'll cover everything from teamwork and DIY projects to picking the perfect dining table for your space. We'll take a look at bedrooms built for intimacy, and I'll share tips and tricks I use with my own family to foster empathy and understanding. By the time you've completed the therapeutic work in the pages that follow, your home will be a haven for everyone living there, and it will look stunning, too.

So whether your aim is to turn the guest room into a communal space or find a better flow in the living room so everyone can actually enjoy movie night,

I invite you to settle in and get ready to design a more beautiful and fully realized home that will make everyone you live with feel happy, safe, and confident. Imagine a world with device-free family dinners, relaxing hang-out spaces, and stress-free entertaining, and that's the Communal Domain. Welcome.

ABOVE: Creating a conversation pit with a sofa and two facing chairs allows for ultimate connection in the living room.

PREVIOUS PAGE: Leaving the exposed wood finish inside these open shelves provides a warm contrast against the white built-ins. This is an easy way to give your shelving visual interest without incorporating loud patterns.

FOLLOWING PAGES, LEFT TO RIGHT: Incorporating transom windows in spaces with high ceilings allows even more natural light to flow through. • Higher vaulted ceilings in a dining room call for a statement light fixture. This linear chandelier accommodates the volume of the ceiling and provides ample ambient lighting for the dining table below.

communicating your feelings

When I was a therapist and clients came in for couples and family therapy, I noticed there were two main running themes: communication breakdown and lack of empathy. As I developed my method for my interior design clients and we worked on uncovering their purpose for a communal room, the same themes surfaced. The partners or families would complain about how they couldn't decide collectively on what color the room should be painted or what type of sofa would fit best for their functional needs. Cue the design therapist, *me*!

I found it quite easy to put on both my therapist and designer hats to solve their "paint points." (That's my interior design twist on "pain points." So clever, I know.) Oftentimes, as we discussed the design problem, I would help them communicate more effectively by secretly deploying all of my communication tips and tricks to get them to hear each other, understand where the other was coming from, and reach an equitable solution.

At the end of the day, we all want to feel acknowledged. And positive communication skills, when used consistently, help with that. Having the right skills to express ourselves allows others to better recognize our feelings. Otherwise we're asking the other party to become a mind reader, and that isn't fair. The key to great relationships at home starts with taking on the responsibility for expressing yourself. Let me show you how.

Thanks to the large-scale windows in this living room, the natural light doubles as a decorative accent during the day as it interacts with the wall-hanging plants.

If you're hanging lighting in front of artwork, consider how they will interact with each other. In this dining space, the white pendant doesn't take the focus away from the painting, leaving the artwork to be the statement piece.

When I would hold therapy sessions and ask how a client was feeling, I would so often find myself on the other end of a blank stare. It wasn't because they were withholding, they just didn't know. That's why they came to therapy! So I needed to give them word tools—specific ones. I mean, hammers only work for nails, and screwdrivers only work for screws. If you're not using the appropriate tools, then your DIY projects just won't work. It's the same with words. That's why it's important to build up your emotional vocabulary. It is not enough just to say you are feeling sad, mad, glad, or bad. To foster empathy in your listener, it helps to be as specific as possible. The more we know how to clearly convey our feelings, the more the other person is able to respond and meet our needs, and that's the name of the game. We're all looking to have our needs met and to meet our partner's needs. With super precise word tools, empathy is established, our hearts and minds align, and each party is more receptive to negotiating a problem or issue.

For your next Home Therapy tool, check out the chart on the right for a list of feelings you might experience on any given day.

THE FEELING MOOD BOARD

Naming the exact feeling that you're experiencing can help you move through the emotion, so you don't get stuck. Use this helpful tool when you want to explore your feelings and build your emotional muscle. I've organized the words by domain, but note that you may feel these emotions anytime and anywhere in your home.

Individual

Feelings you might experience when you're by yourself

Empowered
Confident
Important
Responsive
Grounded
Thoughtful
Appreciative
Assertive
Terrified
Anxious
Uncertain
Hopeless
Insecure
Embarrassed
Ashamed
Victimized
Disappointed

Organi- zational

Feelings you might have when it comes to dealing with your things

Aware
Respected
Supported
Proud
Energetic
Satisfied
Valuable
Secure
Overwhelmed
Neglectful
Disoriented
Incompetent
Defensive
Helpless
Bashful
Guilty

Communal

Feelings you might experience around other people, especially loved ones

Open-minded
Empathetic
Intimate
Worthwhile
Cheerful
Cooperative
Affectionate
Faithful
Rejected
Stonewalled
Jealous
Blamed
Critical
Bitter
Vindictive
Irritated
Skeptical

Renewal

Feelings you might have at the end of your day

Intelligent
Vibrant
Creative
Jubilant
Radiant
Reflective
Focused
Inspired
Depleted
Fatigued
Insignificant
Discouraged
Bewildered
Ashamed
Self-deprecating
Disillusioned

Table Talk

Now that you have the basic words in your toolbox, you can build up to deeper communication. Warning: This will require you to be vulnerable and honest. Also, be prepared to listen. I know it's not easy to dive right in and start a meaningful conversation, especially with your significant other. At one point, I didn't know how to do it either! This is a learned skill, but once you have it, doors open and stress lifts. I spent a decade studying interpersonal skills and learning the craft of positive communication before I felt confident and comfortable starting a hard conversation. I don't want you to have to go through thousands of hours of practicing like I did, so I condensed all my learning into a handy paint-by-numbers script you

HINT

Even if you're single, live with a roommate, or have a conflict with someone you don't live with, you can still apply this. Try inviting the person over to your home instead of meeting at a coffee shop where it is noisy and full of other people's conversations. You will demonstrate that you're okay being vulnerable, and the invitation will be seen as offering an olive branch. This can make the other person feel less defensive and more open so you can both come to a mutual understanding.

can use to start your own conversation. Although you can apply this checklist to any situation, because this is an interior design book (and because I deal with partners who can't agree on design decisions all the time), I've used an example of partners who disagree on the aesthetics of their home for my script.

1. Decide on a specific time, date, and location for the conversation to take place. I like the dining room table. Dining rooms are not used as much as other rooms, and they're positive and neutral. This will allow us to trust more and be vulnerable. Store your feelings vocab words here in the credenza or cabinet to take out for "talks."

2. Sit down and before anything else, thank the other person for showing up and being willing to talk about the topic.

3. Remember to wear your "business partner" hat. Imagine you, your partner, family member, or roommate are part of an organization or a company. You have the shared goal of the company succeeding.

4. Have the feelings vocab words handy. When you are having difficulty expressing yourself or listening emphatically, point to a few words that best describe your emotional status.

5. Start each sentence with "I feel x because y. That is why I. . . . What I need is. . . ." (Describe your behavior or reaction to the conflict or problem or issue.) Don't play the blame game.

6. For the listener, first repeat what the other person said before going into your own feelings and description of what happened.

For example: "I hear you telling me that it was hard for you to speak up when I was ranting and raving about how ugly the couch was." Don't make assumptions!

7. If emotions get heated, take a break. But always designate a specific date, time, and location to come back and decide what the next steps are. (I recommend a fifteen-minute break.)

8. Stay on topic. It's easy to throw a bunch of other things into an argument, but that's too much to tackle. Unless the conflict is about the kitchen sink, don't throw it in.

9. Try not to win. It's not a courtroom to present evidence. It's a mediation. You'll never get anywhere with your "proof," so no need to bring out Exhibit B or shaming the

other person with I told you so's. If you get stuck, just come back to, "I hear you and I see you." How can I help you?

10. Once you've expressed your feelings and shown empathy, ask the other person how they would want to solve the design problem. How intensely do they feel about this design option? Or how against it are they on a scale of 1 to 10? If one person feels more strongly, can you negotiate and have the person who feels more strongly make that decision, and the other person make a decision about something else that is important to the room as well?

Remember handwritten notes? I keep a box of them handy so I can stay in touch and strengthen connections with loved ones.

DESIGN TIPS FOR PARTNERS

Here are a few tips for you and your partner to consider as you start therapizing your home together!

Decide on a color palette together. When you have two different styles, agreeing on a palette will immediately lend your home cohesiveness and take some of the guesswork out of what to buy for your home. Color palettes are ideally made up of three colors, so start with three you love and then add in two accent colors to play with throughout. And remember the 60/30/10 rule: Aim for 60 percent of one color (wall) and 30 percent of a secondary color (drapes) and 10 percent of a third color (decorative objects, like pillows). Then dot in your two accent colors (a ribbon of black is always grounding). But the real reward is the psychology—think of team colors! Colors put people on the same team and bond them. It will make shopping fun when you look for "your" colors together.

Get under the hood of your aesthetics. Having worked with countless couples, I've seen some patterns along the way. We tend to think of design choices as a matter of taste, but remember how we tag our experiences on to our homes? I had husband/wife clients where the husband grew up without much, and once he was able to buy his own furniture, he was determined to purchase heavy, sturdy items that signified quality and wealth to him—solid wood and leather meant luxury. His wife grew up at the beach and

wanted to feel beach vibes no matter where she lived. But you know what we learned? Heavy materials can also be beachy! Once we went under the hood we were able to find common ground.

Make a mood board together. This is a fun activity you can do together! Sure you can share Pinterest boards, but I love the visceral gathering of fabric and texture to place on a

board and see how it all works together. The best part? Because it doesn't cost anything, this low-stakes team-building activity makes it easier to reach a no-pressure agreement.

ABOVE: This homeowner wanted a sophisticated kitchen while keeping it family-friendly. These schoolhouse stools paired with the modern fixtures and appliances strike the perfect balance. These choices achieve sophistication while making it feel like a space the kids can live in, too.

OPPOSITE: Wall-hanging plants will thrive best where they can receive natural light. Next to the window in this dining nook was the perfect place to hang these terracotta-potted beauties!

know your conflict personality

I've learned so much about my Aries personality (yes, I believe in this stuff *and* science) in psychological terms. As a ram, and the first of the zodiac signs, I pretty much lead with my big ideas. And by lead, I mean ram them through with my horns at full speed. It's no surprise that I was attracted to a Taurus (a bull who is much more methodical and slower than I am).

In a relationship, there is usually one person who is fast moving and the other slower to warm up. A classic example is the needy partner who wants commitment and their counterpart who is digging their heels in. The pursuer constantly chases a partner for the ultimate profession of love they desperately need. The distancer tends to need more time to process emotions, and it might appear like they are cold. In reality, their social emotional processing is just different.

So how does this all relate to home design? Well, if you know there are certain trigger moments in particular spaces in your home, prepare a spot where you can have an outlet. The pursuer might need an individual spot to call a friend or relative. Meanwhile, the distancer will need an "away" area, to process all the emotions that were just thrown at them.

Accent paint can play a huge role in creating designated spaces without adding walls. Pick your favorite color to define an area for specific uses and then use accessories and wall décor to fill up the space!

The Family Check-in

When I was in practice, one of the first things I would teach families in therapy was to set up a family meeting. Every week my first question to them would be, "How did your family meeting go?" Many times they would flash me an embarrassed smile and say they forgot. Usually they would call family meetings only during times of major change like moving or switching schools. But then I had my star families or couples who made the effort, developed a habit (that took just three weekly meetings), and turned their sessions into positive outlets they looked forward to each week. It became easy to achieve emotional peace during the week because they knew there would be a designated time and place to feel safe and express not only good feelings but also bad ones, ugly ones, and everything in between.

Without a designated spot to put all these feelings, how do we even remember to express them? It's like public speaking—without a stage or podium, people wouldn't know you wanted their attention. Here are some basic rules for setting up your own meeting:

Don't underestimate the power of your ceiling. Intentional architectural details like this ceiling alcove transforms this dining room into an elegant space for hosting guests for any occasion.

GROUND RULES

- No devices
- Only one person talks at a time
- Parents are the CEOs so they will listen to reason but have the final say

FAMILY MEETING STRUCTURE

1. Decide on a day, time, and location (I suggest the dining room as the communication hub). Once a week is best.

2. Keep the first meeting under fifteen minutes. Subsequent meetings can be thirty minutes. Short and sweet is best!

3. Start each meeting with a positive note about each person attending. Are there any personal wins or achievements this week?

4. Make note of any important dates or scheduling items (carpools, sports schedules, class schedules, etc.) or upcoming event preparation.

5. Then discuss conflicts or problems in the past week that need to be addressed. Use the Feeling Mood Board (page 181) to draw out feelings if you there is silence or an impasse.

6. Remember that everyone at the table is on the same team. Remind everyone that any problem can be solved together with good communication. The results may not be perfect but there are always options! So do your best to communicate clearly and empathize with a kind and tolerant heart.

7. End the meeting with a fun activity like ice cream or an outing to the park.

Table Talk

The phrase "come to the table" is a negotiating term for a reason. Tables are for coming together and forming authentic alliances. If you think about it, so many of our important life events involve sitting together eating and talking. We grow up around our tables. Whether that means weddings or holidays, toasts or announcements, hope or dream declarations, memories are made sitting at tables with friends or family drinking, reminiscing, and laughing. But what if our table could bring our relationships to the next level? What if the dining room could do more than just host celebrations (and become a place to throw backpacks and scatter markers if you're some of us)? What if it could be a conduit to genuine, positive communication? Using home therapy, this table can be a place for breakthroughs.

I'm certainly not recommending that you turn family dinners into therapy sessions, but I am suggesting that you can use your dining table as an emotional container to hold your communication. Hear me out. Imagine you're in the car and you get into an argument with your spouse. Instead of shelving it and practicing avoidance or allowing it to escalate into something bigger, call a fifteen-minute pause to decompress. Then plan to meet at the dining table at 5:00 p.m. This automatically makes the other person feel more contained because they know they're going to have a follow-up to say what they need to get off their chest. There's an orderly plan to have a reasonable discussion. Everybody feels supported, acknowledged, and seen.

Voilà! Relationship elevated. Dining table as communications hub/container.

But what about the table itself? What about the design stuff? Don't worry, I got you.

When you are shopping for dining tables, or any table for that matter, it's helpful to think about what kind of conversations will take place there. Are there going to be many conversations happening all at once? Or do you want that space to foster meaningful conversation between two or three people? Do you want a small bistro table for dining al fresco with your partner by candlelight on summer nights? Or do you dream of a large rectangular table with bench seating and many chairs for hosting Sunday brunch with your besties or family? What about comfier chairs so your family can linger longer over home-cooked meals? Or maybe it makes sense to forego the dining table altogether and make an all-in-one island/table in the kitchen? When you base your design on your ideal relationship dynamics and how you want them to grow, you are practicing design therapy.

Let's take a deeper look at the table options for the kind of conversations you strive for in your dining room. Keep in mind:

1. Function. What do you want to accomplish at this table? Will it need to do double duty and provide WFH space? Should it be large or expandable to accommodate your whole extended family?

2. Shape. Make note of the space in which you want to fit the table. Is it out in the open with no constraints? In front of a bay window? In a long rectangular room? Does it have to fit in a weird corner nook?

3. Flow. Think about getting to the chairs with the table there. Is it cumbersome? What shape would let you slide into the chair or bench most easily? Does the shape of the table allow the rest of the room to feel easy-breezy, or does it block like a traffic jam?

Arched doorways provide a soft invitation into this dining room. The similar wood tones on the furniture and the art drama create cohesion and further that warm, welcoming feeling.

ROUND AND OVAL

PROS: These tables break up very linear spaces to create better flow. For example, if the dining room is rectangular and the credenza is also rectangular, then a round or oval table adds softer edges to balance the boxy design and vibe.

With little kids, parents don't have to gasp every time they run around the room because there's less risk of taking an eye out on a sharp corner.

You can choose a pedestal base so that chair placement is much easier. This is the best option for bench and banquette dining corners.

CONS: You lose a little more surface space so it becomes a cost-benefit analysis to land on the perfect table.

FOR SMALLER SPACES: If you like a curved aesthetic, but have a smaller space, you may want to choose a round table because ovals tend to take up a bit more room. Even though you lose some surface area in your small space, you can maximize seating because the round edges are conducive to squeezing in that one extra person who stopped by for dinner at the last minute.

Oval tables can range from traditional wood to the mid-century modern Saarinen Tulip–style table. Aesthetically, it depends on what you are drawn to balanced with what kind of intimacy and conversation you want to achieve.

RECTANGULAR AND SQUARE

PROS: Most dining rooms are rectangular so these tables fit the best!

They're great for large gatherings because they have variable widths and lengths for different room sizes and often have leaves to pull out and extend.

This shape has the most variety of styles, ranging from modern to farmhouse to traditional. And since the tables are highly structured, it's easy to find chair styles and pendant lights to fit.

CONS: The corners can be dangerous for small children and will need to be childproofed if young kids are around.

They can look harsh in a very square room with square furniture. I suggest a round light fixture and round centerpiece to offset this.

FOR SMALLER SPACES: Like oval tables, rectangular dining tables require more space along both the length and width than round and square ones. Square tables seat up to four people and work well in smaller spaces. They provide a more intimate conversation platform without worrying about losing surface space like you would with a round tabletop. Also, all four people are equidistant, which makes for good conversation for everyone around the table. No one is too close or too far away.

Rectangular and square table styles vary widely: from traditional cherrywood to farmhouse rustic to modern high-gloss. Here again it is up to you to decide what kind of vibe you want in that space— formal? informal? highly structured?—with the goal of achieving the most comfortable and inviting room for good conversation with those you love.

TABLE SIZE TIPS

ROUND AND SQUARE TABLES:

- 3 to 4 feet (36 to 48 inches): seats 4 people comfortably
- 5 feet (60 inches): seats 6 people comfortably
- 6 feet (72 inches): seats 8 people comfortably

RECTANGULAR AND OVAL TABLES:

- 6 feet (72 inches): seats 6 people comfortably
- 8 feet (96 inches): seats 8 people comfortably
- 10 feet (120 inches): seats 10 people comfortably

PRO TIP

Not sure how many chairs will fit under your table? The info above allows for 24 inches per chair, which is the minimum for comfort (you can go up to 30 inches for a more luxurious setup). Make sure to measure underneath the table, between the inner legs, rather than the table top.

RIGHT: Taking time to set the table for dinner, especially on a weeknight, sets a nice intention for the family to gather.

OPPOSITE: Implementing a fun color—like this bold pink—in various ways throughout a space helps make it look more sophisticated and intentional.

MATERIALS MATTER

Materials used for dining tables can also influence the conversation vibe you want in the space.

Glass both visually and psychologically influences transparency. It is also great for darker or smaller rooms because it's airy and the light reflects off the glass.

Concrete is grounding and solid. It acts as a secure anchor and encourages the people gathered around the table to talk more effectively. If you choose concrete, offset it with lighter furniture so the room isn't too heavy.

Wood is organic, authentic, natural, and durable. It feels raw and honest.

Marble is refined and striving. It feels feel stylish, clean, and inviting.

ABOVE: Use pots with varying heights to create a centerpiece of greenery on your dining table.

BELOW: Keeping the benches and dining table white in this nook allowed the opportunity to layer in more colors and textures with the dining chairs and bench pillows.

Pairing a hard-finish dining table with natural-textured dining chairs provides a pleasing visual contrast.

Dining Chairs

When I'm advising clients on dining chair choices, I'm often met with an exasperated look. As I inquire more, I hear about a long history of disagreement between partners about what constitutes comfortable and/ or aesthetically pleasing chairs. Even if there is no partner friction to contend with, my single clients develop analysis paralysis when it comes to dining chairs. My advice is to first have an open mind: no negative thoughts about a chair that your partner loves and that you hate, for example. Second, I strongly urge you to sit in the chair before purchasing. If that's not possible, do a deep dive into online reviews. It is essential for us to feel good in a chair; it needs to be comfortable if we're going to forge connection here. Third, visualize your dream scene of what your dining experiences will be like once you have your new dining room digs. Does the chair enhance and complement that social and relational experience? This will help you decide on a configuration. Do you want arms, armless, or a combination? Do you want a bench and seating mix?

ARMS VS. ARMLESS: Decide whether you want arms or armless. Arms tend to look heavier and can make chairs more difficult to get in and out of (dashing to the kitchen might not be as easy). They are also pricier and often look more formal unless you go with something streamlined like a mid-century modern wishbone chair. That said, if you have long dinner parties (or hope to, once you get new dining chairs), arms might be more comfortable for your guests. Just remember, the arms should be able to slide under your table with ease, so be sure to have at least 7 inches of clearance between the top of the arm and the underside of the table or bottom of the apron.

NEW VS. OLD: Another option is to pair an affordable new dining table with vintage dining chairs. You can either splurge on a set, or you can mix and match for an eclectic feel. Vintage chairs will lend a lived-in look with design depth and sophistication. The chairs automatically make the table more interesting, and it's satisfying to know you curated a one-of-a-kind look on a budget. This is where a high-low design technique shines.

BENCH VS. CHAIRS: For several reasons, I'm a huge fan of having chairs on one side of the dining table and a bench on the other. First, for larger gatherings (or for families with lots of kiddo playdates and singles who love to entertain) the bench can easily squeeze in extra people. Imagine a bench full of five-year-olds happily chowing down on mac and cheese. Plus, it's a space-saver. If your bench doesn't have a curved back, you can set it right up against a wall. Lastly, it fosters a sense of community. Did you notice there was a point when many restaurants suddenly began incorporating benches? Sure, this was to fit more patrons into smaller areas, but it also helped to foster a sense of human coziness in an increasingly digital world. Styles can range from rustic and homey to beachy and modern.

DESIGN TIP

When your dining space is in a corner and you want to create benches but aren't the DIY type, get two settees and place them in an L shape to mimic corner banquette benches. As long as the settee is about 18 inches from the floor (you don't want your knees to bump up into the underside of the table) you will be good to go! A standard table height is usually around 30 inches. Settees are affordable and come in all kinds of styles and fabric prints to make a fun dining statement.

Tale of Two Kitchens

I simultaneously renovated kitchens (as seen on this page and on page 202) for two different clients in the same neighborhood. And guess what? They had the same floor plan, but flipped. So their kitchens were the exact same size, just opposite one another. And when it came to finding their Core Desire and discovering their tastes, it was a complete one-eighty as well!

Feeling the Modern Farmhouse

The parents at this modern farmhouse kitchen love to cook every meal. With all the delivery options and fast food we have at our disposal, I almost thought that didn't exist anymore! They are also wildly busy with their two teenage boys who are involved with multiple sports in a given season. Even with these dizzying schedules, they make eating at home and having dining table discussions a high priority. In addition, their extended family comes to visit them at least every other month.

So you can imagine how important the kitchen is to their family lifestyle. In the original plan, the range was on the island and that cut their meal prep station in half. There was no room to have multiple people meal prepping, especially during holidays when so many people were around.

By simply moving the range to the back wall, it gave me the opportunity to create the ultimate organized, communal meal prep island. While this is an expensive move, I urge you to consider layout above all else; you can always cut the budget in other places. For me, flow and infrastructure reign supreme.

Then we considered the appliances, cutlery and cooking utensils, plates, serving platters, bowls, and more, and found a home for it all. This is where moving the gas range and investing in custom cabinets were worth their weight in gold.

The family reported back to me after their first Thanksgiving and said it was the best and most effortless one ever! Everyone was happier moving around the kitchen and less cranky with each other because they all had space to cook their designated dish. The biggest boon? The two teenage boys now come downstairs willing to help cook and spend pre-dinner time together as a family because the kitchen is so inviting and organized. Now they *want* to help!

ABOVE: Stocking up on natural-looking kitchen utensils can help add visual variety in a neutral kitchen.

OPPOSITE, ABOVE: You can incorporate different handles and pull shapes on your cabinetry as long as they're the same finish.

OPPOSITE, BELOW: If you're aiming for a less cluttered look in the kitchen, you can use fewer pendants over a large island if they come in a wide enough size.

Living on Island Time

On the flip side, this sleek, sultry kitchen with shiny black appliances reflects a completely different communal dilemma. This multicultural family of five desperately needed a dining table and open space to eat.

They are also an avid sports family, and with three kids playing soccer, they often eat on the go. But the clients knew the time with their teens was limited: In just a year their oldest would be heading off to college. So it was time to update the kitchen hub and improve family connection through mealtimes before it was too late.

As with many cookie-cutter homes, there is a space between the kitchen and family room with access to the backyard. Many newer homes don't have the same formal living and dining rooms of yesteryear, but builders still make a nod to these, resulting in tiny, useless spaces. Almost always, homeowners try to squeeze a small dining table in between to eat. Not only does that block the flow, it also makes the dining experience an uninviting afterthought. I've helped clients transform these spaces from twice-a-year spots that don't work to functional home office or playroom spaces.

In this case, the family wanted to eliminate the old, tired dining table altogether, open up that walk space again, and create a gigantic island to double as their dining table. Even though their cabinets were not custom, we were able to make the island work for them in a big way. Unlike the modern farmhouse family,

these clients didn't emphasize storage as much. Instead, they prioritized dining. So the spacing and seating of the island was important for us to measure and get right.

The change was a hit! Since reconfiguring their dining space, they report so much more joy and ease in eating together. Now their haphazard grab-and-gos have turned into stopping and having family dinners at the dining island.

So whether it's a family who uses meal prep as a way to deepen relationships or

a family who uses a huge dining tabletop and island to connect, these are two great examples of how design can help increase positive communication and develop empathy within your household.

ABOVE: Island pendants can often be an afterthought. Make sure you take time to find pendants that shine, as they can end up being the focal point of the kitchen.

OPPOSITE: A herringbone backsplash will rarely let you down. In this instance, the white tile creates subtle texture and movement alongside the white cabinets.

DESIGN TIP

Be realistic with your remodel. You can't always do it all. That's why I suggest putting together a list of communal goals—in order of priority—before starting a renovation or purchasing new furniture.

OUR COLLABORATIVE KITCHEN

When it was time for my kitchen remodel, I had very specific communal goals: My girls and I are part of a national mother-daughter service charity league. We participate in volunteer events throughout the year. From serving meals at the Ronald McDonald house to handing out water at the Susan G. Komen Race for the Cure, it is a great opportunity to learn community outreach. We signed up because I wanted to teach my children that serving others helps you feel confident with your social skills, increases empathy, and is a fun way to get to know new people from all walks of life. So I thought, Wait, why not treat our home as a community as well?

Thus, my communal priority list before I began my kitchen reno went something like this:

1. Improve the flow of the kitchen so that any family member is able to help with a specific task. This leads to confidence and an effortless team feeling. It sends the message that helping each other out is just natural.

2. Incorporate a smoothie station so that anyone can prepare healthy smoothies for the whole family. When the other family members appreciate and verbally praise the person who made the snack or meal, they have positive reinforcement and their brain releases serotonin and dopamine. Then they want to repeat that action to feel good about themselves. Thus, the communal connection between the family members who give and receive is reinforced. Having them learn to take care of others also creates empathy and agency. Service is a big theme in our home, can you tell?

3. Create space so that we can all take turns cleaning up for each other. This way we are collectively investing in each other's success. While cleaning as a group, we learn to communicate with each other and negotiate. The girls may want to switch tasks, for example, or they may need to trade dishwashing days when there is a scheduling conflict. We also do something called "pick a decade"—everyone gets to take turns choosing a song from that decade—so that it becomes fun. Who knew kitchen chores could do that, right?

ABOVE and OPPOSITE: The organic-shaped accessories and décor in this kitchen provide a pleasing visual contrast against the harsh lines of the tiled wall.

trust in the power of play

Get ready for recess! Just as the dining room is a central place for productive communication, the living room is the place to chill, play, and hang. Being social is an important part of staying healthy in mind, body, and spirit, and play is an integral part of the therapeutic process. Not only is it necessary for kids, but adults benefit from shedding their adulting responsibilities and letting all their worries dissipate at home as well.

We often have limiting beliefs about play as a waste of time or a luxury. It is neither. I prescribe some kind of screen-free play (other than the occasional movie night or dance party in which everyone is invested) for at least thirty minutes every day. More on weekends. Depending on your age, that might mean playing with the puppy, pulling out the board games, telling jokes, playing instruments, going to the park, doing arts and crafts, going to the beach or hiking, or simply making mixed drinks from the bar cart in your living room for friends. Play also mends rifts, increases trust, and heightens happiness.

BENEFITS OF PLAY

1. Stress buster: I've mentioned brain health and endorphins a lot. Well, play activates your brain to release endorphins. And lots of them! The more you laugh and have unadulterated fun, the happier vibes you get. Don't you want some right now?

2. Health elevator: Play time aids brain development in small children, and it helps maintain social connection and positive brain stimulation in adults. For older adults, play lowers blood pressure and minimizes depressed moods. While playrooms for children are wonderful portals to the world of imagination, the living room serves the developmental purpose of building social skills.

3. Relationship booster: Play is a state of mind. Once you get together with someone and laugh and let yourself go, your connection becomes more authentic and less judgmental. Compassion fills the space instead. Play even has the power to heal wounds and rebuild trust. In trust lies the start of intimacy. All through play!

4. Memory mobilizer: Classic games such as chess and puzzles trigger our brains to practice dexterity and increase memory and concentration. So the next time you want to grab the remote control, grab a game out of the game basket by your coffee table instead.

5. Expression improver: When we play, we use our words to express ourselves. The more we talk, the more we are practicing communication and social skills. It also teaches cooperation and give and take, which makes us feel heard and seen.

Stay Intentional in Your Play Places

If there is relationship disruption or hurts and disappointments in the home (which happens to all of us), then using play is a surefire way to regroup and start building that bridge of trust again. It may not happen during the first play session, but over time there will be more laughter than tension.

Are you starting to realize you're not having as much fun as you should? Me, too! It's never too late to start. Here are some tips:

1. Form a habit. Remember the positive loop? Schedule play time (yes, add it to your daily calendar) so that it becomes a habit in a play space. Soon your mind will associate that room with all the fun laughter, high endorphin levels, and happy vibes. Plus, consistency builds trust and safety. Everything is a habit waiting to be formed. Let play be your priority habit.

2. Mix it up. Try something new at home. Be spontaneous and invite others to join you. And be sure to turn off devices. I have to hide my phone when I make time for my girls. It is way too easy to check that notification or email that pops up.

3. Make it a date night. If you are on the dating scene, having fun by way of games and enjoyable activities is a great way to establish a positive relationship and bond. Cut through the initial date awkwardness and embarrassment with a game of Anomia!

Molding patterns are unique architectural elements that create special moments in your space. Adding wall décor can help highlight those features.

creating a conversation circle

Nowadays, it is rare that we entertain guests in a formal living room. Whether you have an open great room or a small space that doubles as your living room, consider a furniture configuration aimed at optimal conversation connection by creating a conversation circle furniture strategy.

What I love about this strategy is that it takes away the guessing game of what type of furniture to buy. When you identify the "play" activities that already go on in the space or that you want to increase, you'll automatically know what size sofa you want, as well as the types of coffee table, side tables, poufs, or ottomans.

And once you know what you need, you can factor in the aesthetics. So often we have it backward: We dive right in to aesthetics or attempt to "fit" furniture into the space, and then we try to accommodate our lifestyle into our conveniently sized, aesthetically driven furniture. Reverse that!

Make sure your area rug is large enough to accommodate all the furniture pieces. This intentionally grounds the room.

**START YOUR CIRCLE WITH THE
SOFA:** Put your thinking cap on and
observe the relational dynamics that go
on in your living room. Your sofa will be the
focus and anchor of the conversation so
you'll want to consider the human aspect in
relation to size, fabric, and shape. This info
will guide you toward a two-seater or a
three-seater or an L-shaped sectional. How
many people will want to sit together on the
sofa at a given time? Do those people want
mostly to have cocktails and conversation?
A curved sofa might help with that. Or do
those who use the sofa generally require
deeper seating for nice naps and lounging
during a movie? My magic number is 27
inches deep if you can fit it.

When you imagine material, do you
anticipate lots of activity, snacks, and spills?
Friends who pour wine? Kids who jump?
Then a high-performance fabric sofa might
be a good option. Do you want everyone to
feel warm or cool on the sofa? No matter
which fabric or color you decide on, don't

DESIGN TIP

Use blue painter's tape on the floor
to mark off the dimensions of the
sofa, coffee table, or rug that you
plan to buy. The general design rule
is to allow 30 to 36 inches of walkway
between large pieces of furniture,
or a minimum of 24 inches if your
overall space is small. That means
the distance between the sofa and a
set of two accent chairs on the other
side. Think intimate conversation with
breathing room.

be precious. A living room that functions
like a showroom does not foster the kind of
connection you're seeking.

**MAKE THE COFFEE TABLE YOUR
SIDEKICK:** I view the coffee table as the
quintessential sidekick partner to the main
attraction of the living room—the sofa.
When you think about communication and
growing relationships, the coffee table is
complementary to your sitting experience
because you need a surface to hold your
supplies. Are you and your partner or family
playing board games? Do you need a tray
for the remote controls and gaming devices?
Are you living in a small space where you
use the coffee table to eat? Or perhaps you
fill the table with snacks and drinks while you
entertain?

Round coffee tables are especially
conducive to good conversation and
connection in an intimate setting. You can
use the conversation circle furniture plan
quite nicely here. Plus, these look great with
round sofas. Set all the chairs around the
coffee table and you've got a good thing
going.

Rectangular tables are better for
activities that require more surface area
such as board games or movie nights
where you want to put out a nice snack
spread.

Oval coffee tables are similar to oval
dining room tables: You get the best of both
worlds. They have more surface area but
can fit into smaller spaces than rectangular
coffee tables. Most important, there's
less chance of toddlers and preschoolers
getting hurt on sharp corners, especially if
you use a fabric table with top trays.

NESTING TABLES

Nesting tables add multifunctional surfaces in a space-saving way. Think three tables for three different purposes at one get-together. And when not needed, they can be stacked in one place and function as a side table. I generally like to flank a sofa with two standard end tables, but feel free

CREATE MULTI-MOMENTS WITH SIDE TABLES: Smaller tables are so important to functionality. While coffee tables help with communal sharing, side tables are the key to personal comfort. Almost everyone in the living room should have this convenient surface area for drinks, snacks, books, or playing cards.

LEFT: Plants will always add texture and life! Use different sizes and containers to create interest.

RIGHT: Glass-top side tables provide sufficient display space for all of your go-to accessories.

MARTINI TABLES

I have to admit, I generally don't like to design a room with tiny things. I want substantial, purposeful furniture placement. And sticking a diminutive drink table in between two heftier accent chairs in a small space isn't my first design thought. But after I visited my client's home and saw

to get creative. If one side is conducive to game nights or cocktail hours, then add a nesting table on that side instead. As long as it is the same metal or finish of the other end table, it works!

ABOVE LEFT: Floor lamps are key in providing both task and ambient lighting in those areas you use most often.

ABOVE RIGHT: Having some kind of end table is essential for the sofa—even if it's a mini martini table just big enough for a coffee cup.

DESIGN TIP

The best tiny drink tables in my opinion are pedestal types because they take up the least amount of space.

that she placed a few drink tables in her living room, I was inspired. As a designer, I learn awesome ideas from homeowners who organically design based on their own needs.

MAKE CONNECTION THE STAR: These days, furniture in family rooms is often placed around the shrine that is the television—like it's a star on stage. I intentionally do not have a TV in my family room so as to to promote conversation. If you do, however, need one (or you've decided it will bring your family closer together and draw them out into the central space), then I strongly suggest finding a way to hide it, whether behind mirrors, cabinets, or a painting. Place poufs or a bench in front of the TV to complete the circle rather than letting it cut the circle off. If you've gotten accustomed to the background noise of a TV and it gets too quiet, add a record player or a cool Marshall speaker.

KEEP CHATTING WITH SWIVEL CHAIRS: I can't profess enough love for swivel chairs. After all, they marry great design and functionality. I have countless clients with a combined kitchen and family room floor plan. And every single time I have the privilege to redesign the rooms for them, I add at least one swivel chair. Since the chairs can turn a full 360 degrees, they promote as much social interaction as possible anywhere in the combined space. If you happen to want to talk to someone behind you, you just have to swivel around. No problem!

Of course, if you prefer stationary accent chairs, just angle them as I've done in the living room above. This provides just enough of an angle for the person sitting there to talk to more people in the space, which is the crux of the conversation circle furniture placement strategy.

CLOSE THE CIRCLE WITH POUFS AND STOOLS: The perfect fillers to complete the conversation circle furniture strategy, these seats round out smaller spaces in between accent chairs and sofas. They can be a little offset and still look cohesive, and they're easy to move around. Taller poufs and stools can also stand alone as end tables when not used for seating. Adding these seats creates organic, easy ways to promote bonding and meaningful interaction. And they're just plain fun!

In therapy, I often helped clients learn to face their fears by leaning in to them and holding them for a while before letting go. It wasn't an easy process. Many would get close and then run away as fast as they could. Some others, who were courageous enough to hold on longer, felt completely terrified. It was so much more comforting

ABOVE: Including a mix of seating for your conversation circle allows for a flexible furniture arrangement that can adapt to the activity.

BELOW: If you change up your décor a lot, use a bowl to hold decorative items as your dining table centerpiece. You can easily swap out the items whenever you please.

to just go back to hanging on to the fears and to rationalize that this is just who they were.

It can be a similar situation with our home. There are parts of our home that haven't been working for us—whether that's a terrible floor plan and flow or just a leaky faucet that we haven't repaired. We use many excuses for why we haven't addressed these issues; we're too busy or we don't have enough money or time. We would rather live in disarray than face the fact that we need to be responsible and take care of things for our own well-being.

Placing importance on and respecting our relationship with our home sends the message to our brain that this is a priority. So the next time something comes up, let's start training our brains to reframe a problem. Instead of running away from the fears, we will feel comfortable facing them and taking action.

Entertaining and Relating

If you are in tune with who your guests are and what their relationships are to one other, then you can create a lasting and authentic experience. What is going to make them feel real and vulnerable and make this time genuine? It's less about whether or not to use the cool serving dish and more about connecting with whether you're hosting new acquaintances (icebreaker games), friends from college (put out old photos along with Polaroid

cameras to capture new memories), or a group connected by a common interest (jam together if you all love music). What about a craft activity? Wine tasting? Mocktails? Just remembering what someone is allergic to or if they're on a diet makes them feel comfortable. For me, if my guests walk away feeling bonded, then I have succeeded in my goal of elevated home entertainment.

So put human connection at the forefront and the formalities of what looks good or cool on the back burner. Sure, you should show your guests how much you appreciate them through beautiful aesthetics. But be sure to add another layer by personalizing. How about celebration dinners where we're not marking a holiday but celebrating relationships instead? Can you create a personalized tablescape based on what's been most important to all of you? Use these get-togethers to reach out and serve those who are coming into your home by way of a fun shared memory or notable moment. You'll deepen your connections.

DESIGN TIP

If you know whether you're an introvert or an extrovert you can tailor your entertaining to what's comfortable and authentic to you so you get the most enjoyment out of your get togethers. Take the quiz by scanning this QR code.

SPOTLIGHT
Pretty In Pink

This LA homeowner lives and breathes to entertain in his eclectic 1930s apartment. Like a love letter to the art of entertainment, the bright pink dining room reflects his "hostess with the mostest" identity. Imagine five-hour dinner parties kicking off with 1950s-style cocktails and appetizers, and friends and family talking, laughing, and clinking glasses into the wee hours.

When finding your purpose and relational reason for your dinner, get-together, or celebration, focus on highlights of your relationship with your guests—either collectively or individually. Consider this LA host's next soiree. Say he's inviting his fun, colorful group of design friends. He would start with memorable foods and drinks that remind them all of their last successful styling gig together. He might pull up a playlist featuring each attendee's favorite song. Perhaps he knows this group is into dance parties so he chooses music in that vein. Using the connection of food, music, and memory, the host has set up the ambience and intimacy.

Usually the host of a party or event *assumes* that a theme for a dinner party or celebration will be fun. In reality it may or may not be something the guests will enjoy. Instead of focusing on serving doughnuts from the new, trendy doughnut shop on your block, try to highlight a positive aspect of your relationship with your guests. I've thrown gatherings that range from hitting a piñata to conjure childhood memories one week to a wine-soaked poetry reading

the next. It's all about creating authentic connection to the evening and each other.

It's not unlike group therapy! When I would conduct these sessions, I had to ask myself, based on the dynamics of the group, what would get them to open up and feel comfortable? What would light them up and bring them together? What would make them feel safe enough to let their guard down? The beauty is, if you're hosting a group at your home you likely know their personalities and how they relate to one another. So whether you're re-creating a tapas and sangria-laden dinner you shared in Barcelona, or inviting your childhood friends over for a wacky theme night of a sixth-grade sleepover, imagine what would bring your guests together the most.

Wall-mounted adjustable shelving fixtures allow for flexibility when displaying your décor. If you need more space for a larger item, you can simply adjust the shelves as needed.

SPOTLIGHT
Bright Lights, Glam City

The homeowner of this Manhattan high-rise apartment loves to host brunches, happy hours, and spa nights for her friends. She knows they appreciate beautiful flowers, after-work drinks, and face masks. She's mindful of the fact that her best friends work just blocks away and that her apartment is a great place to blow off steam with creative cocktails after a long day. She's also aware that her crew is big on self-care and personal improvement, so she invites them for champagne and pampering by manicurists and pedicurists. When she found out that her friends were looking to cook more, she hired a chef to teach the group!

This chandelier and fan are in the same line of vision. Making sure they have similar finishes ensures a cohesive look across both spaces.

Hallway Connections

When a client comes to me asking me to improve relationships in their home, I think beyond the living room and dining room to spaces like the hallway. In fact, I often talk about the hallway first. This is the thoroughfare where everyone is coming and going. So it's a prime spot to slow down, take a pause, think intentionally about what you are about to do or say, and interact in a positive way.

You can make it more of a communal space by creating a cozy pathway and connector of rooms. And why not make your hallway a communication conduit? In addition to incorporating elements to revive your senses, include notes, cards, pens, and a small tray to leave messages for others who are walking through the house. It's even a cute way to ask a family member if they want to take a walk with you or sit outside on the hammock at 3:00 p.m.

This is exactly what I suggested this couple do with the hallway leading into their bedroom. They had this beautiful long metal shelf that ran from one end of the hallway to the other, but they felt that the shelf was underused.

So I added invigorating plants, a bench, art, and candles. But most

important, there are cards that say "You are awesome!" on one side. The couple loved the idea of leaving a pen here and writing to each other because—with busy work schedules and two teens—they so often felt like two ships passing in the night. This was another means for quick connection!

ABOVE: Implementing aromatherapy into hallway spaces helps the scent carry farther into your home, providing more opportunities for you to enjoy the health benefits.

OPPOSITE: Art ledges are a more flexible way to display your décor. You can move, adjust, and layer as much as you need.

build
boundaries

In our increasingly digital world, boundary lines are harder to draw. While we might be alone more often, our devices are constantly breaking into our personal space and interrupting us during moments that should be authentic or quiet. At the same time, the open floor plan with a combined living room and dining room has become increasingly popular in home design. This configuration has many upsides—it makes a home feel airy and casual, and you can be social with guests or keep an eye on kids easily. What it doesn't do is delineate boundaries. That means we need to be super clear about the function of the different areas of our homes.

To enhance connection, it is important to differentiate between spaces, and to do so in a way that still looks aesthetically cohesive. The word "boundary" can easily be misconstrued to mean putting up walls and separating yourself; yet boundaries actually increase connections by encouraging individuals to pursue personal fulfillment and avoid resentment within relationships. Healthy, clear rules make everyone feel safe and bring people closer.

A few ideas for dividing open rooms follow.

Using furniture with a smaller footprint makes sure the traffic flow from one room to the next stays clear.

Define with Rugs

Rugs are a spectacular way to define combined spaces because they lend automatic visual cues using physical boundary outlines. Vertical room dividers like screens and shelves can be bulky and run the risk of blocking sight lines, natural light, and people connection. Rugs, on the other hand, help spaces look bigger. By choosing the right proportions for your rug you can maximize your horizontal plane for the best design advantage. Whether you're trying to create a cozy corner with two chairs and a table with a small rug underfoot for playing chess or having a drink, or you're designing a great room with a 9-by-12-foot statement rug to invite people into your conversation circle, rugs help identify different intimate activities so connections are created! And the best part is the secure feeling you get with the parameters of a rug. This design decision separates different activities from one another *and* imparts a sense of calm.

RUG TIPS FOR COMBINED LIVING

Get the colors right. My secret sauce for choosing rugs in the same space (and I *am* the rug whisperer) is all about a balance in color, tone, and pattern. Just like people, you don't want the rugs to fight, and you want them to live in the same family! I like smaller patterns with busy, desaturated neutrals (think a Persian rug in grays, blues, and creams). To pair two rugs together, make the larger the more muted anchor, and then for a secondary rug, pull out one of the main colors and find a more saturated version in another small pattern.

That's what I did in this living room with a muted gray rug containing subtle accents of blue, green, purple, orange, pink, and yellow. Then, I just followed my own rule and pulled the blue out and chose a more saturated, small-patterned rug to set a boundary around the television area. I kept the conversation circle as the star and drew a visual around this Samsung Frame TV to put it into the background along with paintings and bookshelves.

Get the size right. My pet peeve is rugs that are too small for the living room! They end up making the room look smaller, not bigger. When in doubt, it's likely your space requires at least an 8-by-10-foot rug (and sometimes even a 9-by-12 if you have a large sectional or super long sofa).

Get the placement right. Another "don't" is placing the rug perpendicular to the sofa. The rug should run horizontally to the sofa. The front legs of any seating furniture (sofa,

Hanging pendants can help establish division between spaces in an open floor plan.

accent chairs) should always be on top of the rug—ideally 5 to 8 inches. You also want to make sure to leave some negative space. While the goal is to foster a cozy seating arrangement, don't try to squeeze everything onto the rug. If that means swapping a chair for a pouf and leaving just a standout accent chair, so be it! Overcrowded furniture blocks the flow of the room, and you need a good flow to make this an inviting play hub.

Cut Corners

The little bistro area in this multipurpose room is tiny but mighty. I took an overlooked corner of the room and turned it into an adorable snack/beverage station where the family can have a quick afternoon snack together or where the kids can hang out with friends. Previously, this room was labeled as a guest room and went largely unused, but now this mini area makes it a major communication connector. The pendant is an intentional boundary marker giving a clear visual cue that this is the place for food and drink.

DESIGN TIP

Another great thing about creating boundaries in rooms? You are more likely to keep the space neat and also decorate it with interesting visual details that make your overall design that much richer.

Pair a larger accent table with some stools, and you've got a mini dining setup that can be broken down for other uses as needed.

Quarter Off a Quiet Library

Creating a library spot is an ingenious way to invite quiet connections. When the hustle and bustle of the whole family gets the best of you, steal away with one person you haven't felt connected with in a while and enjoy quiet time. Reading a story together is a surefire way to reconnect, especially with an introvert. You can ease into a natural conversation by using low-key and calming activities to lay the groundwork for trust. Once defenses are down and the other person trusts that you are there to understand, listen, and empathize, they will open up to you.

Keep Boundaries Flexible

Is there an unused room in your home? Lucky you! Depending on your floor plan, there might be a basement or bonus room that can be used for more recreation time. To me, this is the mecca for applying communal tools and staying connected. To make this space work for the whole family, I recommend creating boundaries here, too, but also making sure to keep them fluid. Boundaries should be firm but not indestructible (only you know how to strong to make them). You might set up a movie area with a screen, a "play" area with a Ping-Pong or pool table, or a wet bar area for entertaining friends or keeping snacks for kids, but it's great to let these areas expand and contract as lives and needs change.

SPOTLIGHT
Slice Off a Sleeping Nook

It would have been easy to add humdrum cabinets or shelves here, but instead this family decided to create a boundary based on a communal goal. They thought outside the box and decided to turn a hallway alcove into a fun and intimate family connector where their kids could have sleepovers with cousins and friends. This hub is the center of many pillow fights, Lego-building competitions, story times, and, most of all, memories. They knew what was important to them, found an area usually meant for something else, and converted their dream into a reality! Now the kids look forward to all the fun here. Little do they know, their parents designed a space where they are learning important life skills like boundaries, sharing, communication, and connection.

Curtain panels and a shearling rug add coziness to this bunk bed alcove.

DIT: DO IT TOGETHER!

I'm so proud of the bathroom renovation that Travis and I did together, that I get emotional just thinking about it. We went into this DIY with the aim of improving our connection, and it worked! While tiling and painting late into the night, we found ourselves chatting and catching up about parenting and upcoming plans. It was fun! It reminded me of the early days, when life was simpler before we were married with kids.

That said, there were heaps of challenges along the way. First, I wanted it done in a weekend. In reality, it took a month. But that's indicative of our different personalities. I dive right in headfirst and whatever happens, happens. Travis is the opposite. I call him Mr. Meticulous because he's so slow and methodical. Of course this can annoy me, but I've also learned to really appreciate it and how it makes us an effective team. DIY projects test your mental stamina and grit; success requires clear communication, the humility to say "I'm sorry," and a sense of humor. And the result was so rewarding: Every time I look at our bathroom I'm reminded of the love and teamwork that went into building it.

When you begin a DIY, I always encourage bringing in a partner. That extra pair of hands is certainly helpful, but you'll also find that doing projects together really is bonding. Whether you're working on a small craft or a big project, the more you work as a team the more you respect each other's strengths and weaknesses. Here are some tips for getting through a DIY project with your partner:

1. **Have a pre-meeting.** Discuss materials and who is in charge of which aspect of the project. Make sure you are both clear on responsibilities: Who will go get the materials—or will you go together? Will you need to call in a professional like a plumber? What are both of your expectations for how soon you want to finish the project? How important is this timeline? Use your communication, empathy, and playful skills to set yourself up for success. Remember, this should be fun!

2. **Problem-solve together.** There will always be snags in any project. The key is not to criticize each other. Navigate the first hiccup with mutual understanding. So often our first inclination is to get defensive, but this is an opportunity to strengthen problem-solving skills. Focus on the issue and not on who might have "caused" it. Honor and commend each other's worthy skills to overcome it. There are always multiple solutions, and this is a chance to learn together and build up each other's confidence. Remember that you have a shared goal!

3. **Let go of control.** Relinquishing our "always right status" can be hard because many of us feel like we are the best at planning. When someone challenges that, you can either listen with an open heart and mind or act superior and tell them they are wrong. The latter type of put-down can be much more detrimental to a relationship than you realize. And if you let the other person try it their way, you might learn something. This humbling experience coupled with learning

from one another breeds love and respect.

4. Aim to improve. The more you spend time together, the better you get at DIYs. The goal isn't to create something perfect, it's to create something together. Don't worry if you don't get it right on the first try. Practice makes improvement!

5. Celebrate wins. Enjoy what you've accomplished together and look at that achievement as a product of teamwork and a source of shared pride. It will conjure good memories of working together.

Tiling a shower way to the ceiling brings the eye upward, making this smaller shower feel large and in charge.

invest in intimacy

This leads me to the big four-letter word you've been thinking about since this domain began: love. Isn't that where this is all leading? How do you keep love alive? Yes, it might be some magical chemical reaction made of butterflies and fairy tales that none of us quite understands. But all the principles we've discussed, along with gratitude and intimacy, are necessary to keep it flourishing and vibrant.

When I was a young psychology student at the University of Washington, I had a super cool opportunity to work with world-renowned researcher and clinician Dr. John Gottman in the Apartment Lab he created on campus. It was a "bed and breakfast" right on campus that was set up so we could observe couples for a twenty-four-hour period. It was meant to mimic a weekend getaway in which the couples could do anything they would normally do—talk, watch TV, read the newspaper, or watch boats go by outside the picture window. Except we also monitored blood pressure, stress hormones, immune systems, and facial expressions. We then attached these expressions to a wheel of emotions and coded them. I was one of the coders. I spent hours watching couples as the researchers extrapolated data. The result? The team was able to predict with 90 percent accuracy whether or not the couple would last after observing them for only one weekend.

Smaller accent tables make great nightstands for tight spaces.

To a burgeoning psych nerd like me, this was utterly fascinating. The only exposure to therapy I had at that point was a *Joy Luck Club* moment where I cried with my mom and sister in a single emotional session with a nodding therapist. The fact that human behavior could be examined in this way blew my mind. Over the years, this research informed me as I worked with clients and as I began my interior design practice. What I found in my own life is that our homes can help foster successful relationships. Here are some do's and don'ts:

Keep Electronics Out of the Bedroom

We don't have a television in our bedroom, and we charge our phones in the bathroom. In our nightstand we have feelings vocab words instead. We do this because electronics rob us of connections that are so necessary to building up small positive moments, and before bed is the perfect time to practice gratitude toward one other. Phones and computers take precious time away from telling your partner how much you appreciate him or her. Just as a relationship can deteriorate in a "death by a thousand cuts" way, it can become rich by putting small change in the bank every night. And remember, the simple act of looking at each other is important, so make sure the bed and pillows are comfortable enough that you want to spend plenty of time here. The bedroom is a place to talk to each other about hopes and dreams, to connect through shared needs, worries, and visions for the future. These kinds of discussions are the gateway to passion and intimacy.

Hang Sentimental Art

This is a place to hang not only aesthetically pleasing photos and mementos, but also ones that trigger fond memories and put you on a positive discussion loop with your partner. Dr. Gottman found that the ratio of positive to negative gestures and comments in a given moment of a couple's interaction should be 5:1 to foster a favorable outcome. That means you need to surround yourself with positive reinforcement in this sacred space. Imagine wedding pictures, black-and-white photos, drawings, and quotes.

Oftentimes, if the relationship has been neglected, it is hard to just face each other and force connection. Encourage a sense of fun, ease, and vulnerability by displaying art that evokes a warm memory or feeling between the two of you. Perhaps you'd like to hang photos from a special trip or a Moroccan wedding blanket on the wall.

DESIGN TIP

If you're single and dating, make sure your bedroom is a place that could invite love. Set up the bedroom so that someone else could move in easily if that's something you're hoping for.

Don't Steamroll Décor or Functionality

The bedroom will best serve you as a shared space. Fostering intimacy with your partner can be easy at some points in your relationship and become more difficult at other times. So designing a bedroom that is conducive to making partners feel safe, secure, and comfortable is essential for intimate connections.

Even if your partner is disinterested or ambivalent toward design, he or she is undoubtedly still impacted by the color, texture, and function of a room. So don't take their lax attitude as license to design a room entirely to your own taste. Make sure to consider lighting: Do you like to read in bed while your partner goes to sleep early? Did you decide together on a color palette with soft, calming neutral accents so you're both relaxed in this space? Combine neutral décor with something substantial like a metal bed frame to create a balance of feeling both grounded and authentic.

Have an Outlet

Consider adding a yoga mat or meditation corner in case you end up getting into a "dining table" discussion while you're in the bedroom (which I don't recommend!). It will give you a chance to pause if a discussion starts getting heated. If one or both partners are "distancers," they'll need time out even more. (A yoga pillow can do double duty as a lumbar pillow for the bed.) Getting out of bed should be a calming experience, so cozy rugs on wood floors—or even on carpet—add visual contrast and, of course, warmth. They also ignite your brain's chemistry to fire up those dopamine levels and help you relax.

Make Room
for Love

Talking about serious issues in bed isn't very conducive to warm and fuzzy feelings about each other. And slowly but surely your brain binds arguments with the bed and, well, you can see how that doesn't promote intimacy. Instead, designate another place in the house where you can have these intense discussions and arguments.

A house isn't a home until you fill it with love! Based on years of research and teachings from mentors, I've found that these are the keys to successful relationships: communication and connection, playfulness and trust, boundaries and self-care, mentoring and teamwork, and love and gratitude. Using my interior design practice, I've tagged the cultivating of these characteristics to different rooms in the house. The dining room is best for positive communication, the living room for playing, the combined great room a place for learning boundaries, and the bedroom for love and gratitude. Working together on DIY projects in any of those rooms bolsters teamwork and mentoring. If you use your home as a tool to encourage these interpersonal interactions, you will master the Communal Domain in your home.

HOME THERAPY HOUSE
the communal domain

Families who talk and play together, stay together!
Throughout this home, I focused on this family's Core
Desire to connect clearly and calmly with each other.
No more frustrating power struggles, Mom and Dad!
The whole family reveled in fun colors, textures, and
new furniture plans to invite them to spend quality
time together. Creating new narratives with The
Feeling Mood Board and Table Talk script (pages 181
and 182) genuinely helped them utilize their dining
room table and kitchen counter to the max.

PART 4

the renewal domain

An accent wall is a great way to make a focal point in your bedroom. Add art, sconces, or architectural detailing to make it yours.

Now it's time to set up your space for your own self-care. Welcome to the Renewal Domain. You can't replenish from an empty well, and the Renewal Domain is about taking time to nurture yourself so you can maintain the results of all your home therapy work.

Even though I'm an advocate for relaxing and someone who values to the *nth* degree the rituals that go with it, I can't always luxuriate when I want to (hello, three kids?). Therefore, it is important to set up my home so that I can take advantage of any impromptu moments in which to indulge myself. My bathroom is specifically designed for me to relax and engage all of my senses, starting with the skylight.

For many years this space was dark and dank. It was architecturally impossible to let in any more light than was already coming through the side walls, but installing a skylight allows so much natural light to flood in you have to curtail it with shades. Now I enter my bathroom each morning with a smile on my face. I start my refreshing morning ritual by lighting a candle and reciting an intention.

And sometimes when I just need to hide from it all, even if it's midday, I will take a bath to relax. The white tiles and glass reflect the light all around me, while the plants, white oak vanity, and black fixtures ground the overall design. It's my happy place!

I'm constantly thinking about how to support wellness in every room of a home. The key to doing this is to heighten your senses through your décor. After all, the more we indulge our senses, the more connected we are to the present. This leads to a better life, which is meant to be smelled, touched, tasted, heard, and seen. By engaging with sensations, you invite awareness into your day-to-day, helping you refill your internal spring so that you can keep giving to others, expressing compassion, and being thoughtful.

At its core, achieving wellness is about getting off autopilot. Think incorporating small, simple practices like breathwork. So let's slowly wade into the waters of calm and respite. You deserve some leisure time, and the doors to your home spa are opening now.

A chandelier or pendant above your bathtub is such an elegant touch. This is also practical as it provides ambient lighting to encourage relaxation during bath time.

enhance your visual environment

Everything that catches your eye in your home—from color to lighting to art—sends a message to your brain and has the potential to create a positive reinforcement loop. In our increasingly image-centric lives you need to combat negativity from the outside world and control your own environment because you spend a large majority of your time here. Sight is such a powerful sense—you can use it as a mood booster and energy lifter. By applying relaxing and awakening colors to your rooms, harnessing natural light, bringing in fresh greenery, and hanging transportive art, you can enliven this sense and make your home more of a wellness retreat. So get ready to feast your eyes and warm your soul!

Don't under-estimate your bedside lamps! Take the time to find something unique that reflects your style—they can really be showstoppers.

Understanding Color Psychology

Color is powerful and has many psychological benefits when used in design. It can make us feel energized or calm, cool or cozy. While there are some universal associations with hues found in nature—like the blues of the ocean and the greens of trees—we also have many personal associations from our memories and experiences. Seeing color, particularly in vast quantities together (like in a rainbow) or in our homes, is an emotional and visceral experience. Color, and even the absence of color, greatly influences our ability to renew. And it's very individual: While some see lots of color as a pick-me-up, others feel overstimulated by strong hues. I always suggest letting children pick their own bedroom colors because color is not only very personal, it's also an important form of self-expression.

So often in our homes, we focus on which colors to choose and then we get overwhelmed when faced with all of the possibilities. But "what color should this room be?" is not the right question. Instead of diving into blue or white, the Home Therapy method asks that you dive into your own needs. Everything about home therapy is relational, so it's best to focus on questions like:

How do I want this room to work for me?

What color will help me renew?

What color will help me show up for life the way I want to show up?

Do I need to be more energized or more calm in this room?

THE COLOR MOOD CHART

ENERGIZING

WHEN YOU NEED liveliness, happiness, fun

GO FOR reds, oranges, yellows

USE IN living rooms, playrooms, powder rooms, utility rooms, sunrooms

CALMING

WHEN YOU NEED relaxation, introspection, refreshment

GO FOR blues, greens, purples

USE IN bedrooms, bathrooms, dining rooms, hallways, closets

CREATIVITY

WHEN YOU NEED innovation, flow

GO FOR whites, off whites, grayish beiges

USE IN art studios, craft rooms, kitchens

PRODUCTIVITY

WHEN YOU NEED concentration, quiet

GO FOR blacks, grays, navies

USE IN home offices, entryways, laundry rooms

CHOOSING A COLOR PALETTE

In terms of home therapy, any home improvement should be a means to our personal actualization. Focusing on yourself will help you edit down your color palette. Ask yourself, How will this

DESIGN TIP

Remember to discuss a color palette with others who are going to use the space so everyone can be on the same page with a shared vision. This will make the entire design process smoother and set you up for success!

room make me a better person, parent, partner, worker? Will it keep me focused, connected, and happy? Here are other ways to narrow your palette:

1. Explore associations. Imagine childhood inclinations, memories with family members, and times you've felt happy and renewed by color. What were those influential hues? Did your childhood bedroom make you happy? Or a beach house in Maine you rented early on in your marriage? What season in your life evokes the most joy? What colors do you associate with that?

2. Take cues from nature. Imagine your favorite settings from either paintings or real life. Do you feel most at peace at a lake house? In a meadow with flowers? At

DESIGN TIP

Sample paints are totally worth it. Get two, paint them on your wall, and live with them for a few days. You can also paint white poster boards and move them around your room. Just avoid relying solely on printed samples from the store. The actual paint might look entirely different than it does on the swatch.

sunset? Skiing in snowy mountains? Where is your happy place when you close your eyes? That will give you clues to your color palette.

3. Collect fan decks. Head to your local paint store and start familiarizing yourself with each color in all its variations before you write off any particular hue. For example, I'm attracted to colorful yet muted spaces, so I like to find less saturated shades. That means I like to choose from the top of the fan deck and pick the least intense version of the color.

4. Stay within the same color value. The key to choosing a cohesive color palette is to pick colors that all seem washed in the same light. For example, choose either all saturated colors or all muted colors, but not a combo of them. Then add in ribbons of complementary accent colors.

LOW-STRESS COLORS

While I love the idea of colorful walls, rugs, and furniture, the Home Therapy method is steeped in flexibility, and for those who want a low-cost, low-commitment room refresher, here are some fun ways to spruce up your home with the simple stroke of a paintbrush.

DEFINE WALLS AND CREATE ARCHITECTURE. Painting arches or half circles on walls to define a space is an easy way to add depth to a flat wall. My family command center in blush is a great example (see page 187). Define the wall behind your bed with a painted headboard shape in mint green or paint a pale blue bookshelf arch and hang a bookshelf ledge on it.

OPPOSITE: Stools can be used as end tables next to an armchair! They provide plenty of space to hold your book and cup of coffee.

ABOVE: This wallpaper pattern is neutral enough in color to sit back, yet interesting enough to draw your eye.

DESIGN TIP

Color is always changing. Because it is made up of wavelengths of light reflected back to our eyes, it will appear different at various times of day and in particular seasons. Look at your paint swatches on walls in the morning, noon, and night to make sure you like them throughout the day. And really study the color at the time of day you are most often in that space. (For instance, look at colors for the bedroom in the morning and late at night, and colors for the living room in the afternoon and early evening.)

GIVE NEW LIFE TO FURNITURE.
Sanding down an old nightstand or chair is a renewal journey in itself. My dad and I once renewed an old bamboo wicker chair with paint. The two-day project allowed us to reconnect, and we were so proud once the chair was finished.

USE COLOR ON TEXTILES. I like to
"dot" the room in a balanced manner. For example, the sofa can usually hold three to five pillows—in a mix of neutral, textured, and patterned fabrics with a few solid colored ones to balance it out. This mix will add renewed energy to the heart of your space.

USE COLORED TILES. My favorite tile
style is to stay monochromatic in color but use shapes and patterns to revitalize an old shower or kitchen backsplash. Even an entryway floor can be reawakened with an unforgettable modern tile pattern.

BRIGHTENING YOUR HOME

Sunlight is the stuff of life itself. It heats the earth, grows our food, and fuels our circadian rhythms. It's energy and poetry and, on the most basic level, it's the reason we get out of bed. Good lighting, including natural light, beckons us to meet it in the morning, and we rest in its absence at night. You can't separate light from psychology because our eyes and brain chemistry are connected to light. It boosts mood and energy, improves creativity, aligns our daily routine, and keeps us active. It has the power to make us happier, more hopeful about the future, and even more confident.

So it's imperative to study the light in your home and bring more in when there isn't enough. The following pages offer guidance on the types of light your space might need.

THE RIGHT LIGHT BULBS

Choosing the best interior light bulbs for your home is important for the renewal experiences you seek. I recommend LED bulbs that mimic natural light for optimal serotonin and dopamine production as well as for positive eye impact. Here is a breakdown of what to look for:

1. **Avoid eye strain.** Natural light emits balanced color waves so your eyes don't have to strain. Many brands have wellness lines—such as Philips's EyeComfort—to reduce eye strain and increase productivity.
2. **Look for a high CRI.** Light bulbs with a high Color Rendering Index (CRI) will light up objects in their true and natural color. Natural outdoor light has a CRI of 100 and is used as the standard of comparison for any other light source. Finding light bulbs close to 100 is best, but there are great bulbs that have an 80 CRI and work nicely.
3. **Use ribbon lights.** LED ribbon lights are one of my favorite ways to illuminate under-cabinet spaces, open shelving, and glam stations. The wonderful thing about these lights is that they are affordable and easily installed. For a customized, seamless look, you can cut a channel under your open shelving so that the ribbon fits flush in the channel.
4. **Check the temperature.** Measured in Kelvin on a scale of 1,000 to 10,000, color temperature describes the color of the illumination provided by a bulb. The lower the Kelvin number, the more orange/red/yellow the light (like a sunset). The higher the Kelvin, the bluer the light appears (think, your device screen).

HAPPY LIGHTS

Looking for other ways to light up your life? You might have heard of happy mood lights, sometimes called SAD (seasonal affective disorder) lamps, which mimic the sun's natural rays to help fend off winter blues. But these therapy tools do more than just increase serotonin and melatonin in the brain, they can also help with sleep disorders by reorienting your circadian rhythm so that cortisol levels are kept in check and don't hinder your sleep at night. Getting better rest helps you make better choices that align with your goals (from cooking healthy meals to being more productive), which will boost your sense of control, accomplishment, and confidence. Sound a lot like a positive loop? It is! And light has the power to do that.

Centering nightstands in front of a window gives the bed more breathing room.

TIPS FOR USING HAPPY LAMPS:

• The magic number for a happy lamp is 10,000 lux light intensity (the equivalent of afternoon sunlight), which will reset your circadian rhythm and improve your well-being.

• Consistency is key! Start using your lamp in early fall and keep using it until the end of spring.

• Alarm clocks that simulate the sunrise and sunset allow you to choose everything from natural red-tinted dawns with crowing roosters to Denver dusks with lightly chirping birds to guided meditations. It's kinda sci-fi but also pretty cool.

• Switch out your light bulbs with full-spectrum bulbs so you can integrate happy lights throughout your home—in your kitchen, home office, and bedroom.

RECESSED LIGHTING

Recessed lights (also called can lights) are the round lights that are usually installed flush into the ceiling. They provide the broad general lighting we all need to function and perform tasks adequately at home. I can't tell you how strongly I

DESIGN TIP

For renters or apartment dwellers who can't add recessed lighting, a mid-century modern pendant semi-flush or flush-mount fixture with exposed light bulbs can help distribute the light evenly to a room at a farther distance.

SCONCES

You hear me tout using vertical space a lot in this book and here is another wonderful design tool for you to use. Wall sconces can be placed nearly anywhere you need to add ambience or task lighting. They hearken back to the pre-modern age, when fixtures like these were used to hold candles and torches. Here's what I love about them:

LEFT: Using lower accessories on the coffee table prevents focal points—like this tiled fireplace—from being blocked.

RIGHT: Creating a vanity space in your bathroom encourages you to sit and take a few moments to yourself before starting your day.

feel about recessed lighting. The reason nine out of ten of my clients lack recessed lighting is because they believe that installing it would be too expensive and messy. Not true! Buying various task and floor lamps instead can ultimately add up to much more than the cost of simple recessed lighting. Once my clients install this scheme, they are astounded by how inexpensive and seamless the installation process was.

- Sconces can be the perfect architectural detail, especially when mounted on a board and batten wall.

- They can be horizontal or vertical and can provide ambient lighting, which is also called indirect or mood lighting.

- These fixtures are excellent ways to save space in bedrooms. They are also great for task reading lights and accenting design. You can use metals or fun designs to add whimsical or sexy vibes.

- You don't even need to hook sconces up to electricity. By using a hot glue gun and battery-operated LED puck lights, you can add perfect lighting anywhere you want.

DESIGN TIP

Don't rely on sconces to light up your entire bedroom. You'll likely need other lighting as well.

WINDOWS

Clear, uncovered windows are an effective Home Therapy tool that help brighten dark rooms and, in return, lift your emotional health. Try to clean your windows inside and out every six months to let in bright light. Install curtains so that they open as widely as possible and don't block any light. In bedrooms, consider blackout drapery or Roman shades to control the light as needed.

If you have the budget, consider installing windows where they could be useful. Don't let your home's existing architecture create limiting beliefs about what's possible. For more than a decade I wished for more light in my living room, but I assumed a new window would be too costly to have installed. Then one day I priced out what it would cost to add a window. I spoke with several contractors, and I realized it wasn't as much as I had expected! I did a cost-benefit analysis of how much happier the extra sunlight would make me and how differently I would feel in my living room, and I decided to go for it. It wasn't even all that big a deal in the end. The result? It's completely changed how I feel about an entire section of my home. I'm happier, more replenished, and better connected to the outdoors—all because I broke through the limiting belief that this couldn't change. I valued light as a source for renewal and made it happen!

ABOVE: The accessories on the nightstand here pop because orange is the complementary color to blue. Keep your color wheel in mind when choosing accessories!

OPPOSITE: Keep your window treatments simple (or do away with them altogether) so you can let in as much light as possible.

MIRRORS

Add mirrors to reflect the light back into your home. They can open up small spaces into something greater, and you can use different shapes to achieve design goals. Floor mirrors add more reflection and also provide vertical fillers for corners and small bedrooms with no closet. Arch mirrors offer the best of both worlds and can almost feel like a window if placed directly in the sunlight. Round mirrors add a soft touch to a rectangular space, while rectangular mirrors reflect more of the room.

• Want to add some oomph to your gallery wall? Add a vintage gilded-framed mirror and you will complete your masterpiece on the wall with extra light benefits.

• Mirrors with shelves are functional catchalls and give you the selfie moment you need in a pinch before you head out the door.

• Hexagonal, half-moon, sunburst, pill-shaped, and woven mirrors are all considerations for adding a punch of style to liven up an otherwise boring wall.

LEFT: Position your mirror opposite a favorite piece of art so you can enjoy it from multiple viewpoints.

RIGHT: Have fun with your last-look mirror. This woven one adds so much style to the wall.

OPPOSITE: Throw a mirror above the fireplace to help make a small bedroom feel more grand.

SKYLIGHTS

While you can go all out with a skylight that opens to let in fresh air, a fixed one or even a sun tunnel are inexpensive ways to welcome beautiful light into your home. They don't interfere with roof joists and can be installed in an afternoon. Imagine the transformation that just a beam of light can bring to a dark space. If I could, I would put a skylight in every hallway, bathroom, and kitchen. For my primary bathroom transformation, we installed a skylight that has solar-powered shades and can open and close via phone remote control. Looking at the blue sky above (and even the rain pelting the closed glass) always gives me a sense of calm.

Skylights can be installed only on the top floor of a multi-story home or in a single-story home because access to the roof is necessary. If you're replacing your roof, consider adding a skylight at that time.

ABOVE: Counter stools with unique backs are essential furniture pieces when your kitchen opens up to another area of your home.

OPPOSITE: Plants don't have to only sit on your end tables. Get creative with different wall-mounting techniques and floor placements! .

A SUNROOM

Have an unused space that gets lots of light? Turn it into a sunroom or a nature room. If you already have a sunny room that has been neglected, it's time to revive it. This can easily become your favorite room in the house if it's properly nurtured.

Think: a bright, welcoming space where you can relax, reset, and sit among plants and herbs set in front of large windows. Your body will read this as direct sunlight, and the beams will help boost your immune system and regulate your mood, helping ward off depression.

Cultivating Your Outdoors

My secret garden is proof that any space can be transformed into an outdoor respite. I turned a former alleyway into a place of renewal and rebirth. It was easy to add climbing vines, cement posts with planters, and a round wooden pole to hold up café lights. Adding a teak bench and a bistro table and chairs completed the look—along with leafy plants and a $30 wedding arch (bought on Amazon) that acted as a trellis. Lastly, pea gravel contributed a layer of texture and reminded me of the gravel in the gardens of Versailles. As I walk on it, the sound grounds every step I take. I created a space where I can just "be"—allowing me to recharge enough to go back into my individual, organizational, and communal growth.

PLANTS

Cultivating a relationship with your plants is a wonderful Home Therapy tool that will help you practice empathy. For example, if you notice one particular side of a plant growing awkwardly up the wall toward more sunlight, you know the rest is deprived and it needs to be turned or moved to increase its natural light. Becoming adept at tending to your plants' needs will help you feel more joyful and happy at home!

Bringing the outside in with greenery enhances the appearance of your space while also boosting your mood, increasing creativity, and eliminating air pollutants. I know this might be a bit out there for some, but if you want the renewing benefits of plants it's best to bond with them. You can start by naming them, which immediately connects you to your plants on a more personal level. Talk to your plants while you are watering or repotting them. Natalie, my youngest daughter, adores baby talking to our fiddle-leaf fig. It renews and grounds her when she's having a hard day.

Here are more Home Therapy plant ideas:

1. Create a wellness plant ritual. We are all energetic beings, so it makes sense to add plants in a proactive manner to a wellness ritual. Just as a sound bath can

OPPOSITE: In my opinion, you can never have enough plants in a home. Here are two great examples of how plants can pepper a space, by sitting in corners or hanging on walls—inside or out.

increase dopamine and decrease cortisol and epinephrine levels, so can a plant bath. (It's like Japanese forest bathing on a small scale.) Here's how you can set this up for your next relaxing bath:

• Surround your tub with plants. Use stools and benches and countertops to create a full landscape of plants around you.

• Combine crystals with your plants for that extra oomph of energy you and your plants need. You can even put crystals in the soil if you'd like.

• Relax and meditate on an intention while enjoying the visual stimulation of greenery all around you, and don't forget how much purified air you are breathing in!

2. Plant a living wall. Not only will this bring a pop of color and life into the room, it will also help reduce noise levels.

3. Go faux or try dried flowers. Artificial plants—and even painted murals of plants—have similar mood-boosting properties as fresh ones (with none of the stress of upkeep). Your eye registers this greenery and sends messages to your brain in much the same way. And they've come a long way from the days of dusty silk flowers. If you have pets, artificial plants are great alternatives to certain live plant varieties that may be toxic to your animals. They are best used in places in your home that have extremely dim or no natural light. Using dried plants in bedrooms, bathrooms (I outfitted my desert shower with dried eucalyptus and made it an aromatherapy steam shower), and in your meditation corner is an excellent way to dress up your space.

4. Hang an herb garden. Fresh herbs benefit the brain and gut health. Building a

simple herb garden in your kitchen will cost less than $30: Install a tension curtain rod so that it's stable. Plant your favorite herbs in 4-inch pots. Using S hooks, hang the pots on the rod. Done.

Displaying Inspiring Art

Seeing art in your home ignites your imagination and brings back fond memories, which contribute to your self-care, helping you refill your well. If there is an emotion that you need, you can use art as a positive association to trigger that emotion. For those of you who are new

to collecting, know that you don't have to spend a lot of money to enjoy great art in your home.

Photography brings an element of real-life humanity. Photographic images can be very raw, or they can be light and meaningful images of family and friends that elicit a feeling of connection. Move around your home. How can you add uplifting visual stimulation to every room or corner?

CLOCKWISE FROM TOP LEFT: The large-scaled piece is the exact width of the ceiling portion in this space, which defines and anchors the dining room nicely. • Rather than springing for one large piece of art, the homeowners hung two pieces by the same artist. • Leaning art pieces on a sideboard reduces the need for excess accessories and provides just as much of a visual impact as hung art.

OPPOSITE: Art can be simple, like this quiet landscape, which picks up on the colors of the room.

adjust your acoustics

Hearing is a vital sense that connects us to the world around us and helps us to stay present. Understanding speech (whether auditory or through sign language) empowers us to use effective communication. Without it, we can easily feel lost and misunderstood. That is why auditory Home Therapy tools are so essential. When I did home visits with neurodivergent children, I assisted parents in planning where the children could best learn and do their homework. If there was too much echo in a space or if the acoustics were not ideal, the space would be overstimulating. On the other hand, we all, including those with neurodivergent characteristics, need a a certain amount of stimulation to wake up this sensory sensitivities.

In order to address sound and vibrations in your home, you need to think about your layout. The open floor plan, for instance, brings the modern family together, but the acoustics can be the worst! The biggest enemy of great acoustics is a large open space where the sound waves bounce back and forth with nothing to absorb and neutralize them; this is when you get an echo. (You can clap in your room to see if there's an echo.) In an open room, large rugs and fabric-upholstered furniture absorb noises and echoes. Hanging art also helps.

When your sound equipment looks as cool as this, you want to keep it on display so it stays in use.

Here are some other design solutions to help improve acoustics:

1. Special sound-deadening underlayment for wood floors (while wood floors are beautiful, they can amplify footsteps)

2. Low-sone fans in bathrooms

3. Strong kitchen fans and range hood fans that are whisper quiet

4. Drywall with soundproof enhancements

5. Solid core doors

6. Large thick wool rugs

DESIGN TIP

If you want to enhance conversations while maintaining privacy, then removable desk screens or vertical panels can be designed for your space. Think office cubicle panels—but more stylish. They need to have solid, dense fabric for a dampening effect; pretty rattan room dividers will not work. You can even DIY panels with cotton batting, fabric, and a staple gun.

Healing Sounds

Once you've mitigated noise pollution, you can add a calming sound like that of a sound bath, which is not a real bath, but a way of bathing in a meditative sound experience. Sound baths reduce tension, release anxiety, and increase positive internal feelings. The great news is that sound baths are very accessible! You can simply sit in your backyard with your eyes closed and listen to branches rustle and birds chirp for fifteen minutes. Try adding wind chimes and tuning forks to enhance your experience. Just practice slowing down and listening.

Indoors, you can create a digital experience with a variety of apps that play nature sounds like babbling brooks, waterfalls, and rain, as well as music that can be easily played anywhere in the house. You can do this in your meditation corner or in bed before you get up in the morning or to help you fall asleep at night. If you have hearing loss, consider a sound bath bowl, also known as a chanting bowl, or a tuning fork. Set an intention before or after your sound bath experience. Your intention can be as simple as sending love into the world or spending more time in your Individual Domain, while centering yourself and setting new goals.

Sound—or lack thereof—can also help set the right mood. There are now noise-canceling headphones to help you transition into a place filled with only the sounds you desire, as well as pairs that work just as well on your run as they do on your next conference call. Look for alarm clocks that function as sound machines, aromatherapy diffusers, and more.

MUSIC THERAPY

Have you ever heard the saying that music soothes the savage beast? While it sounds Shakespearian, it actually comes from a 1697 play by William Congreve called *The Mourning Bride*. We all have an anxious beast inside of us, and music relaxes our bodies and minds. Listening

lights up neurons between the right and left hemispheres of the brain. It can also aid in neuroplasticity, helping the brain form new connections.

I have a client who was diagnosed with Parkinson's disease. She was told drumming therapy would help so we created a yoga room complete with a drum, exercise bicycle, and meditation corner. This is a wonderful example of how someone invited music therapy into their home; you might benefit from turning a big closet or your garage into a music room for singing, playing piano, or practicing guitar. We still keep a basket of baby cymbals, maracas, and a small drum from my kids' preschool days tucked behind the sofa in the family room to remind us that an impromptu session of drumming and clanging is a healthy, cathartic exercise and stress reliever whenever needed.

DESIGN TIP

The reason therapists have sound machines in their waiting rooms is twofold: The walls aren't always soundproof and they help calm patients before their sessions.

LEFT: The copper and pink tones in the pillows and art are subtle here, but they help establish a calming color scheme for a space meant for relaxation.

RIGHT: Position a mini Bluetooth speaker in your kitchen to help you wake up over your morning coffee.

DESIGNING WITH SOUND IN MIND

Bringing music and other sounds into your home can activate your brain chemistry to stimulate those happy feelings. Here are some ways to design around sound.

1. Create a music space with stellar acoustics. A small room will allow you to control the sound more easily. Cover the floor and walls with large, thick rugs and tapestries to reflect sound waves (audiophiles might invest in prettier reflection panels). Avoid mirrors and TVs in this space, which can cause sound to echo. And move speakers away from walls for the ultimate sound experience.

2. Place a Wi-Fi speaker in your laundry room to pair your once-dreaded chore with your favorite podcast.

3. Hang instruments on the wall or display a basket full of percussive instruments (like tambourines or rainsticks) for easy access and to remind you that music is a great stress reliever.

4. Add framed art featuring musical notes or instruments on open shelving or a fireplace mantle. Just the symbols of the bass clef and notes will trigger the brain to bring sounds of music into your mind.

5. Include a record player on a credenza. For me, a rendition of Fleetwood Mac's "Dreams" melts my worries away!

6. Light fires more often and listen to them crackle.

7. Allow for play time in the communal living room to enjoy the sound of children's laughter (instead of video games).

8. Open a window and invite nature sounds from your backyard (you might hear more sounds than you expect!).

INSPIRATION-BASED MEDITATION

Repetition and ASMR (Autonomous Sensory Meridian Response) are also renewing sounds for many. Because it requires you to stay in the present, chanting can decrease stress and kick-start a positive mindset.

I combine a skin-care ritual with meditation and visualization. The act of sloughing off dead skin feels to me like beginning anew. When I cleanse my face I begin my visualization, imagining I am already living the goals to which I aspire. I apply and rinse my exfoliant and imagine a new self. I nourish my skin with serum and connect with the feelings of already having accomplished my visualization. Then I use a micro-current tool and pair the feeling of vibrations and renewal with a mantra. Your mantra can be anything from *everything is taken care of* to *whatever I do today, I will do it with love,* or even just the word *truth, flow,* or *release.* Find your tension pain spots and focus on them emotionally and physically.

connect with your breath

Let's talk about the foundation of renewing breath. At the start and end of true, deep revitalization at home, restorative sleep is the key.

The Stages of Sleep

Awake time: This is time spent in bed before and after sleep.

Light sleep: During this stage, respiration slows, muscles jerk, heart rate decreases, and waking up is easy.

Deep sleep: This is when your brain flushes waste and slows long brain waves. The body promotes muscle growth and repair (blood flow increases to muscles), growth hormones are released (this is why kids need sleep!), and cells repair themselves (important for skin and hair). Beauty rest is a real thing!

REM: This stage (named for the rapid eye movements we experience) occurs every ninety minutes. REM sleep is most associated with dreaming, and our bodies and muscles immobilize to prevent us from acting on our dreams. Our brain waves are as active as they are when we are awake. Getting adequate amounts of REM sleep is essential for memory and learning. It also helps improve our pain tolerance. During REM, our brain is sorting the day's experiences and emotions into long- or short-term memory. When we lack sleep, our realities skew big time: Everything seems like an uphill battle, good habits are lost, and old habits creep back. Make sleep your top priority.

Dressing your bed with fluffy, lightweight layers will beckon you to sleep and make bedtime a delight.

A Sleepy Bedroom

Here's how to design your bedroom for optimal restorative sleep:

1. Beat the heat. Make sure your room is the ideal cool temperature. Most doctors recommend 60°F to 65°F, depending on whether you are a hot or cool sleeper.

2. Keep it dark. Cave-like darkness is recommended for good restorative sleep, so opt for blackout shades. The darkness reinforces your body's circadian rhythm to start winding down.

3. Invest in a good mattress. Ideally, mattresses should be replaced every eight years. (Every ten years is fine if you don't have substantial slumps, dips, and sinks.) If you have back or muscle problems, consider mattresses such as Purple or Casper, which use special materials to help you maintain good posture while sleeping. If you have allergies, search for hypoallergenic or organic mattresses.

4. Don't forget the sheets. Linen sheets work well in every season, breathing in hot weather and layering nicely in colder months with heavier blankets. Choose what works for you.

5. Add some weight. Weighted blankets are a total game changer—they make you feel surrounded and secure, helping decrease your anxiety. Before I consistently used mine, I hadn't slept through the night since my firstborn was, well, born. Add the many years of battling my partner's snoring, and I was quite miserable. Once I started using a weighted blanket, I was astounded! Did I really feel that renewed? Yep, I did.

TO NAP OR NOT?

Napping isn't for everyone, but depending on your personal circadian rhythm, a nap might be just what you need. Midafternoon naps work best for about 55 percent of the population: those of us who sleep heavily through the night and are neither early birds nor night owls. While we feel most productive in the morning, our energy levels taper off in the afternoon, and we can become foggy and grumpy, reaching for another cup of coffee. A thirty-minute nap between 1:00 p.m. and 3:00 p.m. will revive us even more than caffeine.

Napping helps us to remember things we learned earlier in the day, and we'll be better equipped to draw connections between stored information. Once refreshed, we're able to focus on tasks again, with a nice boost to job performance, and have an easier time staying on the positive loop. It doesn't even take sleep to see the benefits—just lying down for ten minutes can ease stress and improve our mood, restoring our energy for the remainder of the day. This renewal tactic will allow you to show up in organizational and communal ways, too!

Finding Your Signature Scent

There's a reason why the scent of freshly baked cookies wafting through an open house tends to help sell a home. Smell elicits a visceral reaction. It travels faster than sight or sound and finds its way into your olfactory system in strong and powerful ways. When the air we breathe hits our noses, olfactory cells produce a nerve impulse that sends messages to the limbic system. This is the primitive part of our brains that dictates survival instincts and emotion. Therefore, smell can change our brain chemistry and re-create positive experiences as well as negative ones. It can send signals through our nervous systems to wake us up or calm us down—to eat, smile, or become aroused.

Scent is very personal so you will need to decide for yourself which ones inspire possibility for you. I'll share mine:

BEDROOM: I love lavender; it sends spa-like messages to my brain telling it to relax. I spray it on my pillow at night; it's my go-to bedroom aromatherapy scent.

Layer in: a fig candle (it's a natural aphrodisiac), ylang-ylang, and jasmine

BATHROOM: For this room, my favorite is eucalyptus in the form of dried leaves or candles. I also have an aromatherapy shower from Moen, which has attachment capsules for the showerhead in scents ranging from Zen to Sweet Morning.

Layer in: a soft relaxing candle in a cedar, cucumber, linen, or ocean scent.

KITCHEN: I think of the kitchen as an invigorating space and prefer mint in this room, which to me signals "fresh." I use fresh mint as well as candles with hints of mint.

Layer in: small pots of herbs such as mint, rosemary, and chamomile (which look like mini daisies!)

SPOTLIGHT
Soothing Small Space

This tiny bedroom works hard so its owner can relax. The serene color palette in the linens, pillows, rug, pampas grass, and furniture tone down the visual vibe (no worries, the brick wall fireplace is enough of a focal point). Candles and eucalyptus above the bed enhance the olfactory senses. A vintage radio by the fireplace adds to the audio experience. Lastly, textured bedding and tufted chairs add a tactile touch to put you right to sleep.

LIVING ROOM: You want this space to be the hub of fun and delight, so whimsical scents are essential. I love Vitruvi's Pacific blend. It is a refreshing and light coastal scent inspired by ocean waves—it reminds me of a cozy gathering of friends at the beach having fun.

Layer in: bergamot, amyris, basil, lavender, and eucalyptus

DINING ROOM: I am always cognizant of not bringing heavy scents into this room so as not to compete with the smell of the food we prepare and eat. Beeswax candles have air-purifying properties that dissipate negative smells. They can emit a light honey scent that will complement your dining experience. Avoid floral scents in dining rooms, as they definitely fight with food odors.

Layer in: beeswax candles in honey and pear scents

ENTRYWAY: This is one of the most integral places in your home, so you'll want to make an effort to develop a signature scent for this space. Let it signify your intentions to guests and to yourself as you enter and leave the home.

Layer in: Byredo's Vanquish, which has touches of old forest and new flowers sprouting from the ground

WORKOUT ROOM: For a workout, I like something energetic and awakening like a citrus scent. Having a scent that doubles as an air freshener is key. I absolutely adore Le Labo's Palo Santo. It gets me into the mood for a deep post-workout meditation sesh, too.

Layer in: palo santo, cedar and suede, mandarin, amber, and lavender

AROMATHERAPY DIFFUSERS

A diffuser for essential oils is a wonderful addition to a room. Just add two or three drops of your preferred oil and enjoy. In addition to supplying a pleasant smell, aromatherapy oils can provide respiratory disinfection, decongestant, and psychological benefits.

There are SO many aromatherapy diffusers out there to fit any aesthetic or budget. My favorite way to incorporate diffusers into a variety of spaces is to think of them as home décor. So if I want to place a diffuser in my kitchen, I think about the best color and shape that will fit in with the rest of my design. Or if I want one on my desk, I consider the size as there is only so much space there.

Your senses can literally lead to your success! Diffusers are great for establishing positive loops. As your nose talks to your brain about this amazing scent you've introduced, your brain establishes a positive loop to support the habits you're trying to establish in that space.

Want to start a new workout routine? Set a diffuser in your workout space and fill it with an invigorating oil. Whether we realize it or not, scent influences our motivation to grow and renew or stop and stay stagnant.

If your bed is low to the ground, make sure to be consistent and use lower nightstands to keep the room feeling proportional.

SCENT YOUR MOOD

Using aromatherapy as a Home Therapy tool is one of the most affordable and effective ways to combat stress. Anytime I am feeling tired, stressed, or overwhelmed, I grab an essential oil from my purse, apply a few drops to my wrists, and then rub my wrists together. I immediately feel better. I can't think of a better pick-me-up than that! (If you have sensitive skin, mix the essential oil into a carrier oil like jojoba.)

FOR SLEEPING:

Lavender
Chamomile
Ylang-ylang

FOR ANXIETY RELIEF:

Jasmine
Bergamot
Vetiver

FOR ENERGY:

Peppermint
Cloves
Lemongrass

FOR CONCENTRATION:

Sweet orange
Basil
Cardamom

SCENTED CANDLES

I am obsessed with candles—as many people are. And after what seems like a lifetime of investing in these little gifts to my scent sense, I have developed some important criteria to consider when plunking down hard-earned money for that bougie candle you see online:

1. The scent should be lingering and subtle. Scented candles that punch you in the face will not invite you to replenish your soul.

2. Collect a variety of shapes and sizes, but either keep the colors in the same tone family or choose complementary colors. I like the ease of all black and white candles, but muted colors can be fun, too!

3. Consider what you can do with the candle jars after the candles are burned through. If you put the jar in the freezer, the leftover wax pops right out. You can then wash it and use it as a pen holder or even a drawer organizer for small items such as hair bands or paper clips.

4. Consider burn time and quality of wax. Higher-end brands will have longer burn times (usually five to seven hours burn per each ounce candle for a standard size). Also, to keep the air quality high, make sure that the wax is made with natural ingredients.

CLEANSING FIRE

Growing up in the Pacific Northwest, I was exposed to and gratefully humbled by the influence of the Native American experience all around me. From the city named after Chief Seattle to field trips I took to historical landmarks, as an Asian American, I developed a profound appreciation for and a connection to this culture. So when it comes to adopting certain rituals, such as smudging, I do so with honor and acknowledgment to the culture from which they came.

Burning organic and sustainable wood, herbs, or incense in a specific area of your home—especially while you are honoring a ritual or practicing a meditation—can build healthy thoughts and habits.

Here are some ways to add cleansing burning into your routine:

CEDAR symbolizes strength and structure. You can clear your closet or entryway with this wood when organizing your clothes and shoes.

JUNIPER is similar to cedar, but it's more refreshing. So use this in bathrooms or laundry rooms to promote purification.

LEMONGRASS is nice to burn in the kitchen. It is cleansing and provides clarity and focus. This vibrant scent helps you zero in on your nutritional goals.

BAY LEAVES have an essential oil for healing and are an effective mood booster.

GOOD AIR QUALITY

Prioritizing air quality is an important part of home renewal. Run an air purifier during the day to remove particles of pollutants from the air and a humidifier at night to add moisture. They can work in tandem with each other in the same room; just set them at least 3 feet apart. You don't want to inadvertently clog up your air purification filter with the moisture from the humidifier.

If you and your family struggle with allergies or dryness in the air, you'll want to address these issues for optimal wellness at home. When we live with these conditions for a long time without doing anything about them, we forget how they impact our mental health. When you are feeling overheated and dehydrated, you can get cranky and uncomfortable, which does not make you feel productive or interactive. Communication and the processing of emotions are stifled. Because air is a major factor in influencing our body, mind, and spirit, it should not be taken for granted in your home.

COFFEE CLEANSE

If you're looking for a scent ritual that doesn't involve fire, brew coffee from fresh beans. It is a palate cleanser for your nose and will help you reset. Smelling coffee also boosts your brain. In a study, students felt more confident taking algebra tests while a coffee smell was present in the room. Placebo effect? Maybe. Maybe not.

DEEP BREATHING

As a new mom I would stare at my sweet sleeping babies. I noticed how deeply they breathed while they slept or sat up in their bouncy chairs. Their tummies moved up and down, and they stayed present in the moment while learning and observing the new environment around them. That type of breathing is something we forget as we grow older, but reconnecting with it will help you realign and renew yourself.

Over time, shallow breathing becomes automatic. It wasn't until grad school that I became reacquainted with deep breathing exercises and realized how many times a day I held my breath for no apparent reason. What we really want to achieve for our mental and physical state for rejuvenation is to feel grounded and balanced. In this mindset, there is no need to run from our anxious thoughts or sad moods, and it all starts with re-programming our breath. While there is an entire world of breath work out there, we're going to start with the basics.

HOW TO BREATHE (I KNOW, RIGHT?)

1. Close your eyes, sit up straight, and visualize air traveling into your body. Bring your tongue to the roof of your mouth as you breathe in. Notice that doing so helps you breathe deeply but quietly. Don't feel like you need to make big heaves and sighs. It is okay if you naturally have shorter breaths. As you practice and find your momentum you will intuitively know your breathing sweet spot.

2. Breathe out, feeling your expanded diaphragm collapse as your nose and mouth work in tandem. Allow your mouth to release any negativity and mental and emotional blocks. Let go of all limiting beliefs as you sigh out the air.

3. Continue inhaling and exhaling slowly, repeating a mantra like *flow*.

4. To prompt yourself to practice breathing, create a daily event in your online calendar, mark it on a paper calendar, or set a daily alarm in your smartphone. Better yet, schedule a five-minute break a few times a day to breathe. This is a serious habit that will turn your day around in minutes and is so worth the effort, I promise.

FRESH WATER, FRESH MIND

Staying hydrated throughout the day literally helps your body and brain function.

When you are thirsty, it indicates that your body is already 1 to 2 percent dehydrated. But did you know that when you feel hungry, your body may be giving a clue that you actually need to drink? I often tell my girls to have a glass of water before reaching for a snack. And, yep, they quickly quip back, *Mooooom, you need to, too!* Guilty as charged. There's nothing like three young daughters to keep you accountable.

Seventy-five percent of our body is made of water. Our heart is a big muscle and needs to pump oxygen continuously. When we stay hydrated, our heart works efficiently to bring that oxygen to every cell in our body. Dehydration causes our heart to overwork which leads to a variety of heart problems. Hydrating our muscles and joints encourages us to stay active (by working out in that corner gym you created, for example).

I am always aware of how we can maximize our brain function and getting enough water into our body is key. If you tend to forget to hydrate, try carrying a water bottle in a fun design around the house. My girls started doing this and I followed suit. Isn't it great when you learn from others?

I have a glass water bottle with crystals. The crystal-infused water helps me affirm my personal intentions. I feel invigorated and full of purpose with each drink. I am also über-intentional about curating the glasses I bring into my kitchen. Gone are the days of college mugs and mix-and-match glasses from friends and family.

When I renovated my kitchen, I edited down all of our drinkware. Now I only have glasses with aesthetics that please me. They are functional but also act as a visual cue for me to use them. When we are motivated, our habits are much more likely to be repeated.

Moving beyond plain water, you can consider bubbly water from a pretty dispenser (think the soda machine from page 28). And having a coffee or tea ritual is one of the best ways to start your morning. I am obsessed with pour-over coffee. I like to state an intention and, as I pour hot water over the coffee grounds, I imagine good feelings and positive outcomes for the day. Inviting love and

THIS PAGE: Be intentional about hydration with pretty trays or shelves where you can set your cup.

OPPOSITE: Soft materials and muted colors ensure a spa-like experience.

joy into my heart, I visualize healthy conversation and interaction with everyone.

My afternoon or early evening tea ritual is similar. It's when I start to unwind my mind and body for the day. Instead of munching on chips because I am tired, I turn to tea (decaf, of course!). Or, if you're not into coffee or tea, you can start a smoothie ritual for mornings or afternoons.

create a sensory sanctuary

Touch connects us to our own well-being and to others in a profound way. The result? You increase trust and intimacy. As much as our mouth communicates our innermost thoughts through words, touch can communicate our intimate emotions through physical sensations. Research shows that infants who get healthy amounts of physical contact have stronger brain and physical development than those who receive limited amounts. So hug your family more often, hold hands with someone special, get busy with your partner, or lean on a friend while you stand side by side. These small acts add up to major wellness moments.

As for relaxing your muscles through touch, the good news is you can reduce your stress and tension and reinvigorate yourself right at home. No need to head to the spa—instead, let your home be the spa that you use anytime you want.

For this homeowner, yoga became a way of life, and so it made total sense to dedicate a room to the practice. And soon she began teaching it from her home. This is what I love about the Home Therapy method. As you grow and find your Core Desire, it can help you expand and help others find their Core Desires as well!

Exploring the Mind-Body Connection

The connection between the mind and the body can only be activated if we get active and wake up our muscles. There are several ways to heighten your self-awareness with the sensation of touch.

LYMPHATIC SELF-MASSAGE

One way to help get you in touch with your muscles is a type of massage that I always encouraged my clients to try: lymphatic massage, which is a technique you can do to yourself. In order for us to feel good and act well, our immune system must be robust. Part of maintaining a robust immune system is to regularly take care of the parts of our bodies that contribute to it. Lymphatic care is essential.

It's no surprise that sitting all day at your desk can cause stress to accumulate in your neck and back. Start by lightly rubbing the lymph nodes on the neck in order to alleviate stress and leave you feeling calm and tingly.

I sit at my desk taking calls and taking care of design tasks all day long. And these tips really help me:

1. Identify a quiet space with a comfortable chair where you can sit; access to natural light is helpful.

2. Think about your intention—or your Core Desire—and focus on this mantra while massaging yourself as a way to renew and relax.

3. Using the soft pads of your fingertips, move with a slow and light pressure along your lymph nodes. This is a delicate massage to get the fluid under your skin and just above the muscle flowing. You don't want to press too deeply.

4. The valves that prevent backflow of blood move slowly—six to twelve times per minute—so keep that in mind as you move your fingers up and down your neck slowly in one direction, not in circular motions.

5. While massaging your neck, repeat your intention mantra. Visualize and let the fears dissipate. Invite those good feelings in!

6. Be sure to hydrate with something refreshing, such as water with lemon or watermelon juice, to help the lymphatic system flush out toxic fluids.

PROGRESSIVE MUSCLE RELAXATION

Progressive muscle relaxation (PMR) is a cognitive behavioral technique I have used with clients to reduce anxiety and stress. To use this stress reliever, bunch up your shoulders, tighten your neck muscles, and clench your fists—you can even make a face if you want to or curl your toes. Then let everything loose and let out a deep sigh. Repeatedly tighten and loosen your muscles, either all at once or working different sets of muscles at a time. I have been using this technique on myself and with my kids to help teach them how to relax before bed or get in the right mindset before a swim meet.

It's ideal to find a quiet place to lie down, and make sure you're wearing comfortable clothes. Lighting a candle or

A darker grout color gives white shower tile that extra pop and shows off the pattern you worked so hard on choosing.

incense helps set the mood. The basic idea is to tense and relax specific sets of muscles for a period of time. Start with fifteen-minute sessions. Once you get familiar with the technique, even a five-minute session can significantly release your stress. That's why I love progressive muscle relaxation: It can be used anywhere, anytime.

Jenny is a design client who struggled with deep anxiety. She found herself obsessed with thinking about past conversations and things that happened at work. When I was helping her redesign her home office zone, she mentioned that she felt like her muscles were constantly tight. After going through her Intake Form, it was clear she wanted to feel liberated from anxious thoughts about work. She wanted to feel confident and have the ability to tell her mind to "shut it" when it was running in circles. So in addition to adding pretty plants, calming landscape art, and a Wi-Fi speaker to stream relaxing piano music, we decided she needed a strategy to practice progressive muscle relaxation every time obsessive thoughts ran rampant.

On her wall grid, we posted a friendly visual cue to remind her to do these exercises. Then we placed a bright yoga mat in a woven basket by her chair. Whenever she felt even the slightest thought or tension, she would take the mat out and lie or sit on it. She'd play quiet music and start the PMR from her face, neck, shoulders, and hands all the way to her feet.

A few months later, Jenny emailed to thank me for helping her with the design but even more for teaching her PMR so she can combat those unproductive habits and thoughts once and for all.

TOOLS FOR MOVING MUSCLES

I am all about giving you easy ways to set yourself up for success at home—especially when it comes to relaxing your body and muscles. Here are four small easy items to have nearby:

• Foam rollers: These are no longer just the black and boring ones you see at the gym. They now come in a wide array of colors, patterns, and sizes.

• Massage tools: These are great alternatives to spending money at a spa for a massage. I especially like the newer massage guns, which are highly effective at releasing tension.

• Jade rollers: I stick these in the fridge so they're nice and cold when I roll them over my face and neck. (Sometimes I forget they are in the fridge, so I keep a cute note on my bathroom mirror reminding me.)

• Scalp massager: This handy tool is light and easy to use. Look for stylish copper-toned massagers.

Keep the tools in a decorative basket or tub, so they stay within reach whenever you need to release tension. I had a design client who wanted to turn an awkward bedroom corner into a place for respite. So we DIYed the perfect side table: I found an oversized basket almost as tall as a hamper. Then I bought an inexpensive round wooden tabletop from Home Depot, stained it, and placed it on top of the basket. This new side table held her foam rollers, massage gun, stretch bands, and travel yoga mat so she could easily stretch and unwind to release all her body tension.

Alter Your Energy

One of my most significant moments with yoga was when I was trying to get pregnant with my first baby. Travis and I had experienced unexplained infertility for five years—we had three years of failed attempts and two miscarriages. We didn't feel comfortable at the time moving forward with IVF because I wasn't high risk and there were no indications of medical problems. We both felt that if it was meant to be, it would happen. But that doesn't mean I didn't feel hopeless and helpless and experience dark moments of despair when my friends were already pregnant with baby number two. One yoga session, the teacher explained how to bend with the pain and uncomfortable pressure instead of fighting it. I had my "aha!" moment. At that instant, my body and mind and spirit aligned 100 percent. I leaned into my pain, shed some quiet tears, and felt a whoosh of relief. I no longer had to fight my depression. I let my mood be. Soon after, I worked through it in therapy and felt freed from hopelessness. I finally reached the acceptance stage of my grief process. I often told my clients the same: Don't fight your negative thoughts and emotions. Without judgment, move with them and accept them. Then decide what you want to do with them.

My point is this: Pressures and stress in life aren't all bad if your home is set up to be your cocoon. The grit and perseverance we eventually learn will give us the support we need through the Home Therapy experience.

Design your Renewal spaces so they beckon you in. Here, we arranged clear containers for tools like cotton swabs and jade rollers and brushes in a modern cup to complement the pretty artwork and décor.

SPOTLIGHT
The Therapeutic Entryway

Feeling grounded, especially at home, leads to a sense of security. You can do this by laying out rugs in your rooms to enhance the tactile sensation for your feet. This couple, who are grandparents navigating a new stage in life, found a way to ground themselves with a foot massage ritual as soon as they step through the front door.

Having a bench, a "last look" mirror, and a console table is a common design for many entryways. But by adding a candle, massage oil and lotion, and cozy slippers, this couple created a coming home ritual that changed their mindset. We also brought in acupressure mats and foam rollers to assist in the massage. They sit on the bench to pause and create a new intention while rubbing their feet, and they use the mirror to look *into* themselves rather than *at* themselves. Afterward, they feel renewed and ready to start their evening.

DESIGN TIPS

1. Light a candle on the console table and make an intention for how you want to interact with your family or self during the latter part of the evening.

2. Sit on the bench and take off your shoes and socks. Clean your hands with hand sanitizer. Take a deep breath and look at yourself in the mirror.

3. Using foot massage oil or lotion, apply pressure to the balls of your feet. Massage those points of pressure as you begin to de-stress.

ACCESSIBLE ACUPRESSURE AT HOME

I have a lifelong struggle with gluten intolerance, though, thankfully, it's not life threatening. My mom and sister also struggle with it. But it is something that was not diagnosed until I was in my mid-twenties. So when I was a child, I dealt with major migraines, brain fog, and GI issues that were chronic and uncomfortable. My mom would often ask our western pediatrician why she was prescribing so much Tylenol for my headaches. It turns out I was getting migraines from all the gluten I was eating.

I remember complaining about my migraines to my elders. On one occasion, one of my aunties who was staying with us took one of my hands and opened it up. Then she took the thumb of my other hand and pressed it really hard into the first hand's inner thumb area. She told me to keep it pressed for at least ten minutes at a time, and that would stop my headaches. Little did I know, I received my first lesson in acupressure! How I treasure those nuggets of wisdom from my relatives. I only regret that my own kids do not have exposure to these same cultural experiences.

The following pages outline ideas for how you can experience acupressure in your own home.

Ear seeding: From pretty crystals to 24K gold, generally ear seeds come in the form of vaccharia seeds (little tiny black metal seeds) that send signals to the reflex centers of the brain. They adhere to different acupuncture points or parts of your ear and can help alleviate stress in your body by stimulating your brain. It's a technique that's been commonly used in China for centuries. If you are afraid of needles, this is a nice way to get used to acupuncture.

By following the instructions that come with your ear seeding kit, apply the seeds to specific points of your ear to help you:

1. Relax your mind
2. Calm your nervous system
3. Brain balancing point
4. Hormone balancing point
5. Heart balancing point

Cupping: An ancient medicinal therapy that creates suction on the skin in order to stimulate energy, cupping therapy kits are readily available online. I first tried cupping when I was in my twenties, and I loved it. I felt truly invigorated afterward. The red cup marks on my back looked a little alarming, but knowing that it drew toxins out of me and that my chi—my energy flow—was balancing made me feel like I had superpowers. Luckily, you can try a mild form of this at home: Lightly cupping your face or body to increase blood flow can help decrease fine lines and increase collagen production by bringing blood to the skin surface. This improves lymphatic drainage, too. Let me tell you how.

First, start with a gentle oil like walnut or jojoba or whatever works for your skin type, and apply it to your face. (Did you know there are forty-three muscles in the face that hold all of our tension on a daily basis? Well, I certainly did!)

Second, start with the zygomatic arch (the area alongside both sides of your nose) and gently move the larger cups (from a store-bought kit) outward and down your face. Do this for two minutes, all while keep the cups moving to prevent suctioning. Use the tiny suction cup for your eye area and be careful to not stimulate the skin too deeply and break any skin capillaries. Finish with an ice-cold gua sha and jade roller to close up your pores—a perfect way to complete this treatment.

Gua sha facial: Using gua sha, which is the process of lightly scraping your face with an oblong piece of rose quartz or jade, has healing elements that date back centuries in China. These self-care tools fit beautifully in a bathroom Intention Tray ready for facial stress relief. When I was young, my mom would tell me my chi was "on fire" whenever I got a pimple or canker sore, and she introduced me to gua sha to help calm my chi.

I always keep my gua sha ice cold in the freezer. Natalie loves to use my gua sha on her own face—she did even when she was eight years old—my little beauty queen at work! My favorite stones are jade and rose quartz.

Before beginning the treatment, make sure they stay clean and disinfected and make sure your skin is clean, too.

Use your favorite facial seed oil and start your facial routine with an ice-cold gua sha. You want to rub the stone along your face in a striated movement to stimulate gentle circulation and relieve stress and tension. Lay it flat against your skin and not perpendicular to it, and start from your neck moving toward your face. Then glide the stone under your cheekbones where there are acupressure

points you can massage. There is also a point right in front of your ear that you can massage. Under your eyes are important, too. It is super important to glide the tool and not drag it.

Crystals: When I was little, I loved collecting crystals because of how pretty they were! Little did I know that their energy worked to align my body, mind, and spirit. Each crystal has a different meaning and is a creative and organic tool that will help you renew yourself in the moment. I hold them in my hand as I make deliberate intentions, or I carry one in my pocket as a tactile reminder to stay present and positive. Plus, they are easy to find and use, and very inspiring. Display them on your bookshelves as a stylish accent. I even put them in my plants to give them some energy so they can then bounce energy back into my home as they grow. You can get started with any crystal kit and enlarge your collection over time.

Get Moving at Home

Staying active is also an important piece of wellness. We need to make our home conducive to moving in order to help trigger our brains to produce endorphins. Because any kind of movement requires an active mindset, I find it helpful to keep an inspiring quote or reminder on the nightstand Intention Tray so when I wake up I know what I need to do for myself. Pre-planning is key to success!

You don't need a ton of space to incorporate a few simple movements into your day. Here are some of my favorites:

TAI CHI: Growing up with lots of extended family who came from Asia to visit and stay for months at a time, I learned and observed a lot about ancient Chinese culture and wellness. One favorite was tai chi, a martial arts technique that emphasizes slow movements, deep breathing, and meditation. The gentle exercises are ideal for times when you don't have access to gym equipment or if you are injured and need something mild to still get your body moving. Reciting an inspirational mantra is ideal with tai chi. And full disclosure, my sister and I used to get SO embarrassed when our relatives would get up early in the morning and go outside in our backyard to do these exercises. Now? My kids and I watch Marvel movies like *Shang Chi,* which make tai chi movements so cool! Funny how your perception and appreciation of things change as you mature. Sorry, aunties and uncles, you were cool back then, I just didn't know it!

STRETCHING: This is such an overlooked yet essential part of our wellness routine at home. Besides drinking a glass of water in the morning, getting out of bed and stretching your muscles is the easiest way to wake up your mind. It doesn't require anything but you! Do you remember that DIY side table I made earlier (page 290)? That client reports she stretches at least 75 percent more now that the table is easily accessible. She starts right when she wakes up and stretches again before bed.

YOGA: A strength-building exercise method, yoga can help your circulation, de-stress your mind and muscles, and assist you in developing gratitude and fortitude. There's certain to be space in your home—whether it's an unused corner of the bedroom or family room—for an attractive basket that can hold a yoga mat and a few blocks. In fact, a patterned yoga mat can even blend into a room design with cohesive colors.

Pops of bright colors by your bedside give you a fun visual to start your day.

Open vertical shelving for towels and accessories immediately creates a spa-like atmosphere. Each visit to your bathroom will feel like you're on vacation.

Take It to the Tub

When I was seeing clients as a therapist, one of my go-to recommendations for stress and emotional relief was a good warm soak in the tub (for those who had a tub).

Warm water increases circulation in your body, boosts your adrenaline, and stimulates all of your senses. With this stimulation, you become more aware of yourself and of how your body reacts to the warm water—feeling your cheeks flush, for example. At the same time, as the water whooshes over you, your mind relaxes. When your mind relaxes, the negative loop in your brain has a chance to stop, and the positive loop can step in. Well-stocked bath caddies support this process. My favorite bath caddies are ones made of teak or live edge wood slabs because they look organic and raw. Anthropologie has some great ones that I buy for my clients. Some have a slot for iPads, books, and, of course, wine or a glass of sparking water.

Here are essential items to keep in your caddy:

1. Epsom salts infused with rose petals, essential oils, and crystals or herbs such as crushed amethyst, eucalyptus, and dried chrysanthemum

2. Life-changing book to take your mind on a journey or to transform your thoughts

3. Soft scented candle to infuse the air so your nose can trigger your brain to make new grooves

4. Body scrubber like a sisal bath brush, agave exfoliating cloth, or sea sponge

5. Soft washcloth and your favorite facial cleanser to wash your face

6. CBD and chamomile body oil to massage your stressed muscles

7. Eye mask

8. Shaving oil and a razor

9. Glass of wine if you like!

DESIGN TIP

Grab a bunch of Baby Blue eucalyptus and, using jute string, tie it to your showerhead. When the steam builds up, it releases the eucalyptus scent into the air.

TRUE CONFESSION: I'm a person who was born with the passion to lead (yes, Aries), and it's not my nature to always rest. In fact, I am writing this conclusion in the wee hours of the night. But I have learned the value of resetting myself so that I work smart and not hard, and I avoid spinning my wheels. Remember that Home Therapy is as much a practice as it is a design method, one that can make you feel stronger and happier in your calm haven, as it does in mine. My hope is that you can use these Home Therapy methods to discover ways to feel confident, less stressed, and overall more joyful with yourself and others.

May your time at home be calm and calm be your home.

the renewal domain

For decades, the bathrooms in this home were ill functioning and dark. The family just lived with it. Finally they broke their limiting beliefs and embraced the fact that they deserved more for themselves. As a result, the newly designed renewal areas are arresting and transformed from the inside out. New tiles, lighting (including a sun tunnel), flooring, and cabinetry revived their hope for starting their day right. Now family members can gain the serenity they seek after a long day working hard at home and school.

Resources

I've gathered my go-to brands and stores that I love to support and that carry my Home Therapy tools. Enjoy!

FOR MATERIALS

Appliances
Cafeappliances.com

Cabinets and Hardware
Semihandmade.com
Rejuvenation.com
Urbanoutfitters.com

Paint
Sherwin-williams.com

Plumbing
Brizo.com
Deltafaucet.com

Range Hood Fans
Zephyronline.com

Tile
Fireclaytile.com

FOR RUGS
Thecitizenry.com
deKorliving.com
Loloi.com
Luluandgeorgia.com
Rugs-direct.com
Wayfair.com

FOR WALLPAPER AND WALL DÉCOR
Amazonhome.com
Cindyzell.com
Etsy.com
Farrow-ball.com
Minted.com
Rebeccaatwood.com
Shelfology.com

FOR WELLNESS ITEMS
Aesop.com
Saintholiday.com
Verilux.com
Vitruvi.com
Youthtothepeople.com

FOR GENERAL DÉCOR
Amberinteriordesign.com
Anthropologie.com
Containerstore.com
Crateandbarrel.com/kids
Elsiehome.co
Hawkinsnewyork.com
Jennikayne.com
Nickeykehoe.com
Rebeccaatwood.com
Serenaandlily.com
Thesill.com

FOR FURNITURE
Alignmentshome.com
Cb2.com
Crateandbarrel.com
Crofthouse.com
deKorliving.com
Earl-home.com
Eclecticgoods.com
Shopgaragecollective
  laguna.com
Luluandgeorgia.com
Potterybarn.com
Serenaandlily.com
Westelm.com

FOR BEDDING AND LINENS
Blockshoptextiles.com
Thecitizenry.com
Parachutehome.com
Potterybarn.com

FOR LIGHTING
Build.com
Circalighting.com
Rejuvenation.com
Schoolhouse.com
Serenaandlily.com
Target.com

FOR WINDOWS AND WINDOW TREATMENTS
Calicocorners.com
Theshadestore.com
Wovnhome.com
Veluxusa.com

FAVORITE STAYS
Airbnb.com
Localhaus.co

MENTAL HEALTH RESOURCES

At the heart of this book is an important message: Take care of yourself. Here are my favorite tools for alleviating anxiety and finding my center:

calm.com
helpguide.org
verywellmind.com

Acknowledgments

When I started writing this book, the world was about to enter an unnerving state of chaos and uncertainty. More than ever, we needed our homes to be the ultimate therapeutic environment. As hard as it was to write and photograph a book during such a topsy-turvy period, I am grateful for every person who believed in me and the Home Therapy method. If it hadn't been for that wonderful support system, this book simply wouldn't exist.

Clients, designers, and homeowners: I'm forever grateful to you for allowing me to come into your homes and "therapize" your spaces. Your hospitality and generosity will never be forgotten.

Angelin Borsics: I'm not only proud to call you my book editor (whoa!) but also my friend. Your unending support, design knowledge, and editorial expertise was just the right medicine for a newbie author like me.

Ali Harper: You are the Yin to my Yang, or shall we say Travis 2.0? If it weren't for your Type A personality to get every shot right, I am not sure we would have the stunning images in this book. Thank you for being a warrior throughout the shooting process and leading the charge, never giving up on getting that perfect shot to show what Home Therapy means.

Sara Tramp-Liggoria: Your effortless approach to photography really highlighted my biggest project yet, The Home Therapy house. I'm especially grateful for how well you captured all the specific organizational tools I used in the home.

Emily Bowser and Ginny Branch: My two amazing master stylists, without whose tenacity and dedication I wouldn't have survived the photo shoots. While I could have styled the shoots myself, I knew I needed extra support to ensure each shot was truly exemplifying the Home Therapy method. And you both did that and more!

The Clarkson Potter team: Thank you to everyone who helped make this book "arresting," especially my new biblio-family at Penguin Random House, including Jenny Beal Davis, Jen Wang, Terry Deal, Kim Tyner, Jana Branson, Allison Renzulli, and Andrea Portanova. I believe that the Universe provides, and I couldn't be more grateful for all of your hard work and excitement to share this book with the world along with me.

Kim Perel: Wow. What can I say? I am the luckiest author ever to have you champion my work and passion. You meticulously walked with me every step of the process and helped me articulate my method to the publishers and beyond. Your patience and all-encompassing literary expertise were invaluable. I love you, Kim!

Emily Henderson: I am so appreciative of your advice and encouragement on making a book during an uncertain time. You gave me the mental clarity to push forward! Thank you, Em!

Shab Azma and the team at Arc Collective: Thank you for continuing to be my angels. Your creative energy and alignment with my passion gives me the confidence boost when I need it the most.

For everyone on the Home Therapy team: You guys rock! I sincerely couldn't have done it without your tireless efforts and energy in making the Home Therapy book a reality. I

appreciate all that you do and what you bring to the table for Home Therapy every day.

Karen: Your guidance and mentorship has given Travis and me the blueprint we needed for our marriage. We are forever grateful.

Brian Patrick Flynn: You gave me the courage to seriously pursue my dreams as an interior designer. Not only are you an inspiration for design, but you are the most kind, generous human being as well. Plus, you are funny AF.

My family: Thank you, Mom and Dad, for never letting me give up on my dreams. Yes, you had your doubts like any responsible Asian parents would, but when the rubber hit the road, you let my creativity and passion soar.

Gloria, my consummate editor since you were ten years old and my dear sister, you are the best gift mom and dad have ever given me. Honestly, this book should be dedicated to you for all the grammar you have corrected for me, including even my pronunciation of *saal-suh*.

To Travis, Rachel, Emily, and Natalie: I don't have enough words to describe my love and appreciation for you. Simply said, you are my therapy at home.